Laura
Jesus ♡
this I know...
Grace, Rick Lawrence

W9-BUF-347

"Yes, yes, yes! I want to be invested in the kind of youth ministry that Rick writes about, where the only thing that matters in my heart and on my schedule is being thoroughly attached to Jesus and helping kids establish this same life-defining connection. If all I did for the next 10 years was pass along this book to hungry youth leaders, I would have a fruitful decade."

—DAVE RAHN, Senior Vice President and Chief Ministry Officer for Youth For Christ, and Director of the MA Program in Youth Ministry Leadership at Huntington University

"My college students have read and reread this book so often that their copies have worn covers. That's a potent indicator of a book that is meaningful. Rick Lawrence has captured the essence of why we get involved in youth ministry in the first place—to faithfully follow Jesus and help others to do the same. I am excited for this update of one of youth ministry's best books."

—TERRY LINHART, Chair of the Department of Religion and Philosophy at Bethel College, Indiana

"Well past halfway through the chapters of my life, I'm still trying to dislodge from my brain the flannelgraph childhood images of Jesus hovercrafting in his pretty blue robe across a glassy bit o' blue. The longer I walk with Jesus, the more wonderful and mysterious he gets. In this book, Rick calls us to run arm-in-arm with teenagers—to the epicenter of that mystery, that person, that incarnate child, that troublemaker, that up-ender, that ultimate rescuer."

—MARK OESTREICHER, Partner, The Youth Cartel

"JCYM is an emboldening wakeup call to youth ministries and churches to root deeply into the raw and powerful person of Jesus Christ. Drawing from a vast resource of personal experience and honest reflection, as well as the sharp insights of several leading voices in youth ministry today, Rick Lawrence reminds us that the best ministry techniques are ineffective without the centrality of Jesus. Anyone who cares about transferring faith and leadership to the next generations needs to learn from the metaphors, the practices, and the simple truths of this important book."

—KEN CASTOR, D.MIN., Assistant Professor of Youth Ministry, Crown College

"A classic that re-pivoted youth ministry eight years ago promises to continue its explosive revolution in this totally rewritten and unleashed release. Rick Lawrence yokes a solid biblical focus to theological sophistication which is then distilled into simple truths and creative apps that show what happens when Jesus is in first place—all of life falls into place and no youth any longer need feel misplaced, displaced, or out of place."

> —LEONARD SWEET, Bestselling Author, Professor at Drew University and George Fox University, and Chief Contributor to sermons.com

"Since September 16 of 2006, my life mission has been to join Father in calling youth ministry to a singular focus on his beloved Son. My specific focus, though incomprehensively important, is incomplete. My focus on the ascended, enthroned, and all-glorious Son needs the other strand of a double helix—a focus on the incomprehensively important life of Christ in the flesh. More than anyone, Rick Lawrence embodies that other strand. Father has raised Rick up in our day to spread the aroma of the Son among teenagers and the adults in their lives. I cannot exaggerate the importance of *Jesus-Centered Youth Ministry*. It will be required reading for every class I teach in youth ministry. Its message clearly is at the heart of what the Spirit presently is revealing to youth leaders—for the glory of God."

> —RICHARD ROSS, PH.D., Professor of Student Ministry, Southwestern Seminary (RichardARoss.com)

"This book is the youth ministry equivalent of Vince Lombardi's famous locker room back-to-the-basics speech, where he reintroduced his players to 'a football.' With insightful theological framing, Rick invites youth workers to start with what really matters—not a bad idea given the dearth of theological thoughtfulness that seems to exist at the frontlines of youth ministry these days. And just for the record—it's amazing how practical a book can be when it is anchored in unshakeable truth."

—MARV PENNER, Executive Director of All About Youth, Head of the Canadian Center for Adolescent Research, and Associate Staffer at The Center for Parent/Youth Understanding

MOVING FROM JESUS-PLUS TO JESUS-ONLY

J.

JESUS CENTERED
YOUTH MINISTRY

RICK LAWRENCE

FOREWORD BY
CARL MEDEARIS

YouthMinistry.com/TOGETHER

Jesus-Centered Youth Ministry
Copyright © 2014 Rick Lawrence/0000 0000 3376 9992

All rights reserved. No part of this book may be reproduced in any manner whatsoever without prior written permission from the publisher, except where noted in the text and in the case of brief quotations embodied in critical articles and reviews. For information, email inforights@group.com, or go to group.com/permissions.

group.com
simplyyouthministry.com

Credits
Author: Rick Lawrence
Executive Developer: Jason Ostrander
Chief Creative Officer: Joani Schultz
Editor: Rob Cunningham
Copy Editor: Stephanie Martin
Art Director: Veronica Preston
Cover Art: Jeff Storm
Production Artist: Brian Fuglestad
Project Manager: Stephanie Krajec

All Scripture quotations, unless otherwise indicated, are taken from the Holy Bible, New International Version®. NIV®. Copyright © 1973, 1978, 1984 by International Bible Society. Used by permission of Zondervan. All rights reserved.

Scripture quotations marked (NASB) are taken from the New American Standard Bible®. Copyright © 1960, 1962, 1963, 1968, 1971, 1972, 1973, 1975, 1977, 1995 by The Lockman Foundation. Used by permission. All rights reserved.

Scripture quotations marked (THE MESSAGE) from *THE MESSAGE.* Copyright © by Eugene H. Peterson 1993, 1994, 1995, 1996, 2000, 2001, 2002. Used by permission of NavPress Publishing Group.

The website addresses included in this book are offered only as a resource and/or reference for the reader. The inclusion of these websites are not intended, in any way, to be interpreted as an endorsement of these sites or their content on the part of Group Publishing or the author. In addition, the author and Group Publishing do not vouch for the content of these websites for the life of this book.

ISBN 9781470714192
10 9 8 7 6 5 4 3   20 19 18 17 16

Printed in the United States of America.

DEDICATION

To the thousands of youth workers who've journeyed with
me through the eight-hour Jesus-Centered Youth Ministry
experience, and have floored me and encouraged me and
brought me to tears because of your insights. Thank you.
The greatest treasure in life is a kindred spirit.

ACKNOWLEDGMENTS

So many have contributed so much for so long to make this work a reality that it's next-to-impossible to list them all. But some must not be missed...

- My youth ministry team at Group/Simply Youth Ministry is amazing—every one of them. This rewrite of *Jesus-Centered Youth Ministry* would never have happened without Andy Brazelton's ridiculous suggestion (and passionate advocacy), Jason Ostrander's unguarded support and leadership, Rob Cunningham's deft editing, Jeff Storm's brilliant reworking of the cover, Veronica Preston's expert touch on the interior design, Stephanie Krajec's determined shepherding of the production schedule, Stephanie Martin's rapid-fire copy editing, and Brian Fuglestad's high-RPM production work. So many moving parts, so little time...

- My life and perspective have been profoundly impacted by the leadership of Thom and Joani Schultz over my almost three-decade trajectory at Group Publishing—thank you for "ruining me for the ordinary."

- My wife and kids are used to my sometimes-cloistered life as a writer, but this extraordinary effort included a good chunk of the holiday season of 2013, when I was out of commission and unavailable. Because they believe in who I am and what I'm about, they sacrificed to make this happen.

- Carl Medearis graciously agreed to write the Foreword to this book before we knew each other very well— through this collaboration, we've become friends. And that's one of the real treasures of this season in my life, one that I'll continue to relish.

- Every single ministry leader who offered their endorsement for this book did so on very short notice, with grace, humility, and conviction.

- To the youth workers from all over the world who serve on our In The Trenches team, your friendship and love have fueled my ongoing passion for the "divine conspiracy" that is youth ministry.

CONTENTS

FOREWORD

By Carl Medearis

I grew up with Jesus. My dad was and is a pastor. My mom played the piano, led women's ministry and Sunday school and, yes, had a bouffant hairdo. I was a PK. I knew the Bible. I understood that "going to church" meant (by definition) Sunday morning at 10, Sunday night at 6, Wednesday midweek at 7, and youth group on Fridays. Throw in some picnics, baptisms (in the park), retreats, and summer camp—and there you have it. The life of a PK. And I loved it. Didn't rebel against it. Thought my dad was both cool and important. Thought my mom was the best cook and the best everything I knew. And I was a Christian.

I then traveled off to YWAM for a year of missions. Came back and started a singles group at my church in Colorado Springs. Was a part-time pastor. Got married to the lovely and amazing Christine Lymberopoulos (that's right, she's as Greek as the Acropolis). Had kids and moved to Beirut, Lebanon, as a Christian missionary sent by our local church. Joined the best mission agency in that part of the world: Frontiers. By the age of 30, I had started several youth and singles ministries. I had led small groups that multiplied faster than a pile of wild rabbits. I had started and led homeless ministries, men's ministries, and prison ministries. I was trained. I had preached. Knew the Bible better than about anyone I knew. A true servant of God—and, oh, very, very humble.

In Beirut we were surrounded by wonderful and loving Arabs, mostly Muslims. And it was then and there that I met Jesus.

Rick takes us on a similar journey in this book—from knowing about Christianity to actually practicing Jesus. We might be Bible whiz-kids, but do we actually know the biblical Jesus from Nazareth? The passionate Jewish leader, teacher, communicator, healer, and friend from the region called Palestine? Not the version from Tulsa (no offense if you're from Oklahoma), but the real Jesus. The one who mystifies. The one who speaks in parables so we "won't fully understand." The one who never answers questions and teases us with bits of truth at a time, never divulging the whole story. The one who both personifies an even kinder and gentler version of Mr. Rogers and his friendly neighborhood and then, WHAM, calls people names that if translated into modern English wouldn't be fit to write. Again and again they asked, Who is this man?

And do we follow his model today? Oh yes, Jesus had a model. A style. A way of doing things. Just because he was God in blue jeans—I mean, in a robe—doesn't mean he didn't have strategies. When we think of ways and means, we think of Paul. But what about Jesus? Why did he send his disciples out in twos? Why ahead of him? Why the specific instructions? Why didn't he answer questions? (I think he knew the answers.) Why, after Jesus confused them, didn't he explain himself, but instead turned to the others still hanging around and asked if they wanted to leave, too? Why? And do our lives and the ministries we lead look like that?

I know for myself the answer to that last question is a painful and resounding "NO." My life looks like Carl. My style doesn't typically emulate that of Jesus. Maybe a bit of Paul or Peter. But not Jesus, the one I say I follow and want to be like. Not sure why, but... it's true.

Rick has done an amazing job of cleverly compelling us back into the arena of Jesus' style and way. The questions he raises and the answers he suggests are right out of Jesus 101. You'll feel horrible one second, because you're not sure how you missed that—and then redeemed the next second as he gently leads you back to the One we all want so desperately to follow. The specific suggestions Rick poses for doing ministry in the way of Jesus are worth the book alone.

This isn't just a call for youth workers to be more like Jesus; it's more specifically a call to do ministry the way Jesus did. It's a book of ideas, strategies, and thoughts that will change the way you think about everything. There aren't many books like that today. This one is!

—Carl Medearis (carlmedearis.com) is author of *Speaking of Jesus: The Art of Not-Evangelism*, *Tea With Hezbollah*, and *Muslims, Christians, and Jesus: Gaining Understanding and Building Relationships*. He founded and leads the Simply Jesus Gathering (simplyjesusgathering.com).

J.

JESUS CENTERED
YOUTH MINISTRY

INTRODUCTION

At the beginning of this Jesus-centered journey, a series of apparently random and disconnected cliffhangers will help set the context...

Cliffhanger #1: In her 10-week devotional prayer resource *Whispers of Hope*, venerated Bible teacher Beth Moore wrestles with the tension Christian people feel as we try to reconcile the static claims of the Bible with the fire hose of information blasted at us by a know-it-all culture:

> "As the information whirlwind swirls around us, we have an anchor in the Word of God. All the peace seekers in the world can't write a better thesis on community living than the Ten Commandments. All the psychiatrists in the yellow pages can't write a better emotional health plan than biblical forgiveness and divine healing. All the financial advisers on Wall Street can't suggest wiser money management than the book of Proverbs. Marital advice? Sexual fulfillment? Guidelines on business partnerships? How to be single and happy? It's all there. Better yet, it never needs an upgrade."[1]

Here Moore is making a case for the Bible as a sort of "user's manual for life"—not at all an unreasonable argument in the Christian community. But this conventional understanding of *what the Bible is for* has brought us to the cliff's edge. This widely embraced tips-and-techniques posture toward the story of God is like a Trojan horse in the church. It has insinuated itself inside our "gates" and released an enemy that has undermined and gutted our commitment to Christ. It not only fails to resonate with young people but, more than that, it's partially responsible for the mass exodus of Millennials and NetGens from the church. Hang with me...

Cliffhanger #2: Donald Miller, author of *Searching for God Knows What,* says he once conducted an experiment in a Bible college class he was teaching—he told his students he was going to explain the basics of the gospel message to them, but leave out one crucial truth. He challenged them to find and identify the missing truth:

> "I told them man was sinful, and this was obvious when we looked at the culture we lived in. I pointed out specific examples of depravity [in our culture]. Then I told the class that man must repent, and showed the Scriptures that spoke firmly of this idea. I used the true-life example I heard from a preacher about a man in Missouri who, warning people of a bridge that had collapsed, shot a flare gun directly at oncoming cars so they would stop before they drove over the bridge to their deaths. I said I was like that man, shooting flares at cars, and they could be mad at me and frustrated, but I was saving their lives, because the wages of sin is death, and they had to repent in order to see heaven. I then pointed to Scripture about the wages of sin being death, and talked at length about how sin separates us from God."

Miller continued on, describing in detail the beauty of morality and the great hope of heaven, and all the incredible things we can experience once we're saved from the consequences of our sin. When he finished, Miller asked his classroom of upperclassmen, all of them well into their journey at Bible college, to identify the missing "crucial truth." And Miller writes: "I presented a gospel to Christian Bible college students and left out Jesus. Nobody noticed..."[2] Hang with me again...

Cliffhanger #3: I was in the room while a nationally known youth ministry expert led a large gathering of training-hungry youth workers through his workshop. After our mid-afternoon break, he told us a guy had come up to him and asked: "You know, all your strategies are fine, but aren't we supposed to be focusing on Jesus in youth ministry?" The ministry expert smiled as he related this encounter, then spread his arms toward the crowd and told us how he'd responded: "Of course youth ministry is about Jesus—c'mon, that's a given!" And a couple-hundred youth workers chuckled and nodded their heads in agreement, affirming and even underscoring the ridiculous underpinnings of the guy's question, eager to move on to more pressing concerns...

Over the Cliff

I know it sounds oversimplified—but the question that seemed so unnecessary to that ministry expert, and to that roomful of youth workers, is actually the most crucial question of our time:

"Aren't we supposed to be focusing on Jesus?"

Well, of course, we say... That's like asking us if it's important for us to breathe. We're already doing that, for Pete's sake. And what's wrong with all that Beth Moore stuff about the Bible having all the answers we need for every area of concern? The Bible is a fantastic "user's manual"! And big deal, so a Bible college class didn't immediately recognize the artful way Donald Miller left Jesus out of his gospel narrative—if I'd been there, I wouldn't have been fooled by that. Whatever this "Jesus-centered" approach to ministry is, it sounds like an unnecessary reiteration. We already have that covered.

At the core of this book is the certain diagnosis that we clearly don't "already have that covered"—that ministry people, by and large, have simply and subtly forgotten that Jesus is at the center of everything. Seven years ago, when the first version of this book was published, one reviewer wrote: "The book is essentially about what the title suggests, building a youth ministry that is focused on Jesus. At first glance this seemed a little trivial and obvious..."

We'd never admit that we've forgotten Jesus in our commonly accepted approaches to ministry and discipleship and Bible study, but our actions are drowning out our words. We need this cliffhanger context because we have unwittingly, even unconsciously, taken Jesus for granted in the rich excess of Western Christian culture. We have functionally moved on to bigger, better things that seem more relevant to the challenges facing the church: new and innovative church structures, ministry approaches that appeal to postmodern and even post-Christian young people, and social concerns that resonate with a globally aware constituency.

If our focus on Jesus is really akin to breathing, then the evidence suggests that most churches, and most youth ministries, are using a ventilator to stay alive. They don't *breathe Jesus* with the force of their own passionate impetus. We'll explore the truth about this impossible reality from many vantage points, because there's plenty of evidence that the impossible has happened in the American church. But more importantly, we'll explore together what a *Jesus-centered ministry* actually looks and sounds and tastes like.

Bored by Everything but Jesus

Almost a decade ago, I was invited to speak at a youth ministry conference hosted by a very large church in the Midwest. The organizers asked me to lead a two-hour pre-conference session for youth workers who wanted something a little deeper, a little more revolutionary. At the time, I was experimenting with a training idea that focused every aspect of youth ministry on a deepening attachment to Jesus. As we explored the possibilities together, a subtle shift of atmosphere grew in the room. By the end of those two hours, that little gathering of 30 or so youth workers had become a runaway worship-train. We were crying and laughing and hungry for more of Jesus. Some people in the room, with many long years of ministry on their résumé, waited in line to tell me a sobering revelation: that they'd never really tasted deeply of Jesus and had never appreciated his height and depth and breadth. I understood exactly what they were trying to say.

So when I emerged from that two-hour training session that had morphed into something much bigger and better, my appetite for Jesus was voracious. What happened during those two hours was messy and unpredictable and... beautiful. Though the session was focused on learning a new way of doing ministry, it had morphed into one of the most powerful worship experiences of my adult life. And with my leadership responsibilities completed, I was free to roam the rest of the conference, popping into as many workshops and general sessions as I could cram in. I listened to many of the best experts in youth ministry that day, all of them brilliant and many of them longtime friends. But by the end of that day, I felt a growing restlessness—a reaction to a *deadening* in my soul as I tried to process the onslaught of ministry "tips and techniques."

As evening settled in, that deadness had spread into a kind of depression, so I found an empty, overstuffed chair in the huge and bustling atrium. I needed to pray, and it was easy to isolate myself in the middle of the throng. In my "cone of silence," I asked a simple question: "Why, why, why, Jesus, am I feeling this way?" Tears streamed down my face, and pain was in my eyes. And then, in one of those moments when the voice of Jesus is crystal clear, he said this to me:

> "You're bored by everything but me now."

I knew it was true as soon as I heard it. Great strategies and tested principles for ministry are fine; they just can't replace the intoxicating presence of Jesus. If you showed up at a cooking class and discovered Oprah was teaching it, you'd probably be less impressed with her recipes and more interested in... *her*. I'd always defined discipleship as a progression that looked a lot like doing well in school— studying hard, growing in knowledge, doing well on "tests." But those things, I realized, now paled in comparison to the undeniable truth: True disciples are captured and carried away by Jesus. They are so "stuck" on him that the natural outcome of their attachment to him is a perpetual willingness to give over their life to him.

It's not that all the tips and techniques I'd been hearing were somehow contrary to a Jesus-centered youth ministry, any more than the cup holders in my Honda CR-V are contrary to its drivetrain. The cup holders are nice, needed accessories, but the car won't move without an engine and transmission. At the time of this unexpected revelation, I'd spent almost two decades as editor of Group Magazine, the world's most popular youth ministry resource. I'd been pointing leaders toward the "cool cup holders" of youth ministry for a long time, and when I was asked to speak, I had a long menu of well-crafted cup-holder strategies to choose from. But that was all over in a moment. From that teary moment in an overcrowded atrium until now, I've never spoken about anything other than Jesus-centered ministry again.

But if a youth ministry of brilliant tips and techniques must now take a back seat to a youth ministry that's inexorably centered around Jesus, what far-reaching implications will this have on what we *do and say and emphasize*? I now have eight years of practice and conversation and experimentation under my belt. I've led thousands of youth workers through an eight-hour Jesus-Centered Youth Ministry experience, and many of them have told me how this fundamental change in focus has first upended and then super-charged everything they do in ministry. In those eight years, my own children have grown up in a Jesus-centered household, and I've seen firsthand the fruits of this focus in their lives. My teenage daughter Lucy must cope with an adolescent challenge that is unusual among her peers: She , like her parents, is also bored by everything but Jesus. And her passion for him has already driven her into a life of mission and outreach to "the least of these."

When Jesus is the center of everything, and when people are drawn into closer orbit around him, fruit happens. That's just the way things work. The rest of this book serves as a welcome mat into a whole new reality. Walk through this door and you'll discover a new way of leading your ministry to students that feels simpler and more purposeful. And along the way, you'll find what your soul has always craved.

Part One
Beeline Imperatives

During the heyday of the "What Would Jesus Do?" fad, I started to doubt the foundations of the movement. The central question of the book the WWJD frenzy was based on, Charles Sheldon's *In His Steps,*[3] is simple: "If Christians are supposed to be following Jesus, why aren't they making more of an impact in their daily lives?" The book's answer was to imagine what everyday life might be like if all of us simply talked and acted more like Jesus. Well, that *would* change everything—especially if we took some kid's Taco Bell burrito, blessed it, and fed a stadium full of people with it. But as far as I could tell from my perch as editor of Group Magazine, the WWJD movement *hadn't* changed everything.

Maybe, I pondered, the Christ-following lives we think we're living are actually disconnected from the real Jesus of the prophets and the Gospels and the Epistles. It's fine to work up my imagined Jesus-response when someone cuts me off on the freeway, but really the whole thing desperately depends on my own intimacy with Christ. I realized something profound: I could miss Jesus entirely by arrogantly assuming that my imagined responses to a partially understood Jesus meant that I was really following Jesus.

"What does 'follow Jesus' mean anyway?" I asked myself. Have I really soaked in the personality of Jesus—pursued him as the most fascinating, enigmatic, lightning-bolt person who ever lived? Am I as passionately interested in him as I'm "supposed to be"? And if he's really all that incredible, why are "supposed-to's" necessary? People who are caught up in a romantic relationship don't have to be told to focus on their beloved; it's hard to stop thinking about the person, actually. No matter what we're doing or who we're doing it with, our thoughts stray to the object of our passion. To use the language of C.H. Spurgeon (more on him in Chapter 5), our life is "beelined" to our beloved. But it isn't the momentum of a "should"; it's that attraction of a lover. There's an enormous distinction between the two.

Teenagers today are staying away from church—or leaving it altogether—because so many of them have been "shoulded" into a relationship with God or the church. If they, instead, had a kind of romantic attachment to Jesus—a passion for him that created a beeline momentum in their life—they'd not only stay connected to the church, they'd also bring a bunch of their friends with them. This book is an exploration of a needed, even a desperate, shift away from conventional youth ministry toward something more transformative. But this journey doesn't start or end with "shoulds." It starts and ends with a continual re-introduction to the Great Love of our lives.

CHAPTER ONE
RESPONDING TO THE BAT-SIGNAL

"Holy Bat-Signal, Batman!" —Robin

When I was growing up in the fuzzy recesses of American history, I'd get off the school bus every day and rush home so I could catch that afternoon's episode of *Batman*—a campy, stilted, over-the-top precursor to the dark and brooding film franchise of today. I can still remember the siren call of the blaring, syncopated theme song: *"Duh, duh, duh, duh, duh, duh, duh, duh, Batman!"* Of course, central to many of that show's storylines was the moment when Police Commissioner Gordon decided to switch on the Bat-Signal, a specially modified klieg searchlight that projected a stylized symbol of a bat on the skies above Gotham City. The police used the signal to contact and summon Batman when they were facing an emergency.

If the church is a stand-in for Gotham City, we're at the point now where we need Commissioner Gordon (Billy Graham? Rick Warren? Pope Francis?) to flip on that Bat-Signal, because the body of Christ in Western culture is facing an emergency. More than 200,000 churches in the United States are in decline. Every year, more than 4,000 of them close their doors for good. The people who've stuck with the church have a higher average age than the general population, and if you backtrack through the generations you'll find that the younger people are, the less likely they are to be connected with a church.

Of course, the United States continues to be a "Christian nation," with 95 percent of Americans believing in God. But the most generous estimate of the percentage of people who still attend church regularly is 40 percent, and the real weekly attendance figure is almost certainly closer to 17 percent (the number pegged by researchers who actually count Sunday attenders). And here's the real kick in the gut: In the space of just five years, the percentage of teenagers attending church every week has plummeted by 25 percent (from 20 percent to 15 percent).[4]

All our conventional responses to this steamrolling crisis have missed the mark. We've tried to become more relevant, more glitzy, more tolerant, more technologically savvy, more flexible, more professional, more sophisticated, more purpose-driven, more comprehensive, more socially aware, more... more. But all our "mores" have done nothing to reverse the trend of disengagement. Even though there are more highly trained, fully resourced youth workers than at any other time in the church's history, the youth ministry landscape looks bleaker than ever before. The evidence is telling us that, despite our best efforts, today's teenagers just aren't getting who Jesus *really* is. And that's the biggest problem facing us, because it's the disconnect that's forming the "cliffhanger" context I described in this book's Introduction.

- The Bible is not, fundamentally, a "user's manual for life," as so many populist Bible teachers assert. It's the story of God, and God has made the point of that narrative (in *both* Testaments) his Son, Jesus.

- The reason Donald Miller could present a Jesus-less gospel to Bible college students without a single person picking up on it is because we've already conditioned young people to embrace a version of the "good news" that's fundamentally about making life work better, not about a grateful, passionate pursuit of the "Scandalon."

- And the reason youth ministry experts, and so many ministry leaders, *assume* we're already focusing on Jesus when we're not is that we're home-blind. We believe we've talked about Jesus so much already that it's time to move on to more interesting, unexplored territory.

The Disappearing Jesus

I was talking with a junior high girl who'd just served as a leader in a churchwide worship experience during Holy Week. She'd spent several days leading people from her congregation into a deeper relationship with Jesus through an interactive devotional experience. The girl was giddy with excitement about the whole thing. I told her I like to ask teenagers to describe Jesus to me—just because I'm curious about how they see him.

7

"So," I asked, "what are some words you'd use to describe Jesus to someone who's never heard of him?"

She scrunched her forehead and tried to wrestle that question to the ground. Finally, she offered this hopeful response: "Well, I'd have to say he's really, really nice."

She was ready to leave it right there, so I asked: "Remember that time Jesus made a whip and chased all the money changers out of the Temple? Does that story change the way you'd describe Jesus?"

She scrunched her forehead again. The smile disappeared from her face. I'd created a kind of intolerable dissonance in her. Finally, with a tone of desperation, she landed on this: "Well, I know Jesus is nice, so what he did must have been nice." I nodded politely and thanked her for thinking through her response. And then I got an idea. What if I asked teenagers all over the country the same question? Maybe I could find some common threads in their responses. So I turned it into a Group Magazine project and hired video crews in five major metropolitan areas to stop teenagers randomly on the street and ask them a simple question: "How would you describe Jesus?"

When I got all the raw footage back, I quickly discovered my experience with the junior high girl wasn't an aberration. Without fail, teenagers' first and favorite descriptive word for Jesus was always *nice*. Here's a sliver-sampler of their comments:

- "I'd describe Jesus as a nice, friendly guy."

- "[He's] a very nice, caring guy."

- "He's, um, nice."

- "Umm... [he's] very nice?"

- "He was a good person."

- "He's a nice, friendly person."[5]

These comments were profoundly sad for me. Sure, Jesus was "nice" to the people he healed or fed or rescued. But he would never be voted Mr. Congeniality. He definitely wasn't nice when he was blasting (over and over) religious leaders or calling his lead disciple "Satan" or an innocent Canaanite woman a "dog" or telling the rich young ruler to sell all his possessions and follow him if that ruler wanted to "inherit eternal life." In Matthew 23, in The Message paraphrase, Jesus told the Pharisees they were "hopeless"—not once, but *seven times* in a row—and then he planted three exclamation marks at the end of that diatribe, calling them "manicured grave plots," "total frauds," and "snakes." In Luke 11:37-45, the good doctor Luke relates this often-overlooked awkward encounter involving Jesus. As you read, think how you'd feel if you were a church leader who'd graciously invited an itinerant preacher to have dinner with your family:

> "When Jesus had finished speaking, a Pharisee invited him to eat with him; so he went in and reclined at

the table. But the Pharisee, noticing that Jesus did not first wash before the meal, was surprised. Then the Lord said to him, 'Now then, you Pharisees clean the outside of the cup and dish, but inside you are full of greed and wickedness. You foolish people! Did not the one who made the outside make the inside also? But give what is inside the dish to the poor, and everything will be clean for you. Woe to you Pharisees, because you give God a tenth of your mint, rue and all other kinds of garden herbs, but you neglect justice and the love of God. You should have practiced the latter without leaving the former undone. Woe to you Pharisees, because you love the most important seats in the synagogues and greetings in the marketplaces. Woe to you, because you are like unmarked graves, which men walk over without knowing it.' One of the experts in the law answered him, 'Teacher, when you say these things, you insult us also.'"

I can just imagine this scene: You're not even eating dinner yet when your invited guest suddenly wipes the polite smile off your face by repeatedly insulting you. Then, still managing to respond politely and trying to give your guest the benefit of the doubt, you innocently ask him if he's aware that he's insulting you. Jesus picks up after verse 45 by effectively saying, "Yes, I'm aware I'm insulting you, and I'm just getting started...."

The point is that a *merely* nice Jesus is no Jesus at all; he's like a declawed version of Narnia's Aslan. And if Jesus isn't really

Jesus to you, your connection to the church will devolve into a fragile cultural commitment, not a real relationship with a real person. My pastor, Tom Melton, once told me: "We don't really believe Jesus is beautiful; otherwise, we wouldn't describe our relationship with him as so much work." We "work at" our relationship with Jesus, and urge our teenagers to do the same, because the declawed Jesus we've settled for *requires us to work* if we want to maintain a connection to him, or worship him, or serve him. The false Jesus of our conventional narratives arouses no passion in students. Their passivity toward him is a natural result of the descriptions they've heard of him—the tips-and-techniques bastardizations of the things he said and did.

A declawed Jesus isn't strong and fierce and *big* enough to walk with students (or us) into the fiery furnaces of everyday life. They're facing big challenges and struggles, and they're looking for someone or something to help them through or give them the courage they need to survive the blows they've endured. Jimmy Fallon landed the best gig in late-night television because he's a nice, likeable, relentlessly upbeat guy, but you wouldn't choose him as your "wingman" if you were walking into a dark alley in a bad part of town. "Nice Jesus" isn't hard enough or tough enough or real enough to walk with teenagers into their own dark alleys of life—and that's exactly why they're asking us to have a deeper, more real conversation about him. Because the only Jesus they've experienced in the church is a Mr. Rogers knockoff, they've naturally turned to "lesser gods" that promise better results, including:

- humanism

- social justice

- drugs and alcohol

- affluence

- video games

- social networking

- sexual experimentation

- spirituality

- sports

- academic achievement

It's clear that despite our best efforts—all our training, commitment, resources, and creativity—today's teenagers just aren't getting who Jesus really is, or they aren't getting *enough* of who he really is, or they're getting, literally, a fake Jesus. As a result, few of them are living passionately with Christ in their everyday lives. According to Dr. Christian Smith's research for the *National Study of Youth and Religion* (youthandreligion.org), nine out of 10 American young people (and their parents) don't have what social researchers call a "devoted" faith. That means:

- their faith in Christ isn't central to their life;

- they don't know the basics of their faith (our own research finds that four out of 10 Christian teenagers say "a good person can earn eternal salvation through good deeds," and almost a quarter of them say Jesus "committed sins while he lived on earth"); and

- they don't see Jesus making an impact in their everyday life—he's merely a church thing.[6]

The Onset of Apathy

Without the passion of a "devoted faith" in Jesus, all that's left is a cultural commitment to churchgoing. And we all know *that* cultural norm is quickly evaporating. The so-called "dropout rate" of regular-attending teenagers is 45 percent.[7] That means almost half of our "regulars" stop going to church once they graduate from high school. We've seen this kind of slide-into-the-abyss before, in post-war Britain. Just after World War II, it was culturally common to attend church in Britain. But today, weekly church attendance is 6 percent, and in many counties it's less than 1 percent. Fewer than 10 percent of British children attend Sunday school. And there are far more "de-churched" people (33 percent) than monthly attenders (15 percent). The biggest declines are among men, young people, and the poor. And here's the final kicker: British pollsters have removed the following census question because it no longer garners a statistically significant percentage: "Do you profess a specific faith in Jesus Christ as the risen Lord?" Church, and an everyday relationship with Jesus, is "off the radar" for Brits.[8]

It's bad enough when there's a populist backlash against the church; what's worse is a church that doesn't even show up as something worthy of backlash. At Group's Future of the Church summit, I was recently with Michael Lindsay, president of Gordon College and former lead consultant for religion and culture for the George H. Gallup International

Institute. In one of his presentations, he made a stunning declaration. It's the first time I've heard a respected American religious researcher describe the church, and a committed relationship with Jesus, as "off the radar" in our culture. During a break, just to make sure he was serious, I asked Lindsay if this was a throwaway line, or if "off the radar" was a carefully chosen descriptor. Our relationship with the church, he affirmed, has devolved from a discipline of loyalty into a quagmire of apathy.

We are following the Brits down a cultural Slip 'N Slide™ into a secularized reality. And they followed the French before them. Lindsay told me: "Charles Taylor at Notre Dame wrote a book called *The Secular Age*—as levels of education rise, we begin to lose our sense of the supernatural. We no longer attribute to God things we can explain. A full-fledged social movement is advancing the cause of secularization in our culture; America is turning into France. The academy and the arts are now setting the cultural agenda. We reward the avant-garde in both of these institutions."

An "off the radar" church that is overshadowed by a growing secularization means that an "all-in" relationship with Jesus is far down the list of teenagers' priorities. Instead, the *National Study of Youth and Religion* found that kids essentially see God as a "divine butler" or a "cosmic therapist." Jesus' job is to be all-in with their needs and their problems, while making no demands on their time, their talent, or their passions. He exists to help them do what they want, make them happy, and solve their problems.

Tim McTague, lead guitarist for the critically acclaimed Christian metalcore band Underoath, sums up this "divine butler" mentality well in a piece he wrote for CCM Magazine:

> "I believe that we... have lost sight of what Christ intended our lives to be and the purpose and faith He gave His life to teach us. As long as we give our 39 cents a day and make it to church on Wednesday and Sunday, we're all good... Whatever happened to the church of Acts, where people would sell all they had and give to the poor and join a body of thousands of people, living a life of prayer, community and servanthood? We now sit, 2,000 years later, in our comfortable homes and Lexuses and mega-church youth groups watching the rest of the world rot away and starve to death. Where is Christ in our watered down, self-serving hybrid of faith and hypocrisy? God exists to pay our mortgages and heal our families, but, when it comes time to sacrifice something of our own, we look away... Somewhere along the way, we decided that being a Christian wasn't a life of serving but a life of being served. God is real and is waiting for a few real Christians to step up and let Him work through them the way He worked through the disciples. But it will cost everything...."[9]

It's easy to "rush to judgment" about this apathetic, self-centered approach to faith in Christ. But the hard truth is that this entrenched attitude is the natural byproduct of the church environment teenagers have been exposed to. Our research pegs the number of kids who say their church has helped them learn that "Jesus is God" at an overwhelming 99 percent.[10] But that's a semantic panacea. The truth is that too few of them are getting a healthy exposure to the barefaced Jesus of the Bible, and too many of them have heard what *we think* about Jesus. But they're not experiencing his raw presence for themselves. According to the NSYR, most American young people believe that:

- God exists, and that this being created and orders the world and watches over human life on earth.

- this God wants people to be good, nice, and fair to each other—as taught in the Bible and by most world religions.

- the central goal of life is to be happy and to feel good about yourself.

- God doesn't need to be particularly involved in your life, except when you need him to resolve a problem.

- good people go to heaven when they die.

- church is just another thing on a to-do list; it isn't a context where they enjoy their closest friendships.

This list of functional beliefs offers no evidence that young people have had a close encounter with the Jesus described by the Gospel writers. In his foreword to Mark Galli's book *Jesus Mean and Wild,* Eugene Peterson writes: "Every omitted detail of Jesus, so carefully conveyed to us by the Gospel writers, reduces Jesus. We need the whole Jesus. The complete Jesus. Everything he said. Every detail of what he did."[11]

For almost all teenagers, Jesus isn't the hub of their life; he's either a "spoke" on their life's wheel (just a church thing) or not even part of the wheel. They have no firm idea of who Jesus really is, why he came, what he actually said, what he actually did, or what he's doing now. And when something happens in their "real" world, they struggle to understand how Jesus is a part of it.

Many likely reasons exist for this crisis of discipleship in the church, but the conventional explanations I hear most often (tied to the "mores" I've listed on page 6) aren't THE REASON. I'd like to suggest this:

Life is draining out of the Western church, and most youth ministries, because we're not setting the kind of growth environment that is conducive for disciples.

Be the Pig

Our challenge is to make the pursuit of Jesus the central, consuming, desperate focus of our ministry with teenagers. This is what an environment dominated by the momentum of an all-in relationship with him promotes and facilitates. The French Laundry in Napa Valley is one of the world's top-rated restaurants. If you work there, the highest honor you can receive is a T-shirt given by the owners to a select few. The

T-shirt slogan "Be the Pig" refers to the difference between pigs and chickens. A chicken might offer up an egg for the meal, but the pig gives his life for it. All-in disciples of Jesus are pigs, not chickens.

The clearest biblical translation of this kind of "be the pig" discipleship is described in John 6. It happened 2,000 years ago on a lonely Capernaum beachfront. When the massive crowds who are following the rock-star Jesus—those who've been captured by his miracles, healings, and teachings—hear him say, seven times in a row, that they must "eat the flesh of the Son of Man and drink his blood" or they'll have "no life in yourselves," they're disgusted and disoriented enough to escape him en masse. And after the dust and noise from their retreat has cleared, Jesus looks at his remaining 12 disciples—also likely disgusted and disoriented—and asks this incredible question: "You do not want to leave too, do you?" And, here, Peter steps to the plate and answers like a pig, so to speak: "Lord, to whom shall we go? You have words of eternal life. We believe and know that you are the Holy One of God."

Peter, like the masses who've just stampeded down the hill, scrambling to get away from Jesus, would likely escape him if he could. But he just can't. He so identifies himself with Jesus that he can't imagine leaving him. He is all-in, a pig not a chicken, and this is what discipleship *really* looks like. Later Paul, another all-in disciple—one of the greatest thinkers and apologists in history—describes his orientation to Jesus this way: "I resolved to know nothing while I was with you except Jesus Christ and him crucified" (1 Corinthians 2:2).

That declaration would make a great tagline to reorient every catchy youth ministry name in the Western world.

I believe youth ministries, and churches in general, have been using a flawed strategy for discipleship that produces chickens, not pigs. I call it the "understand and apply" strategy. It assumes people grow deeper in their faith when they understand biblical principles and apply them to their lives. As we'll explore in Chapter 3, I think "understand and apply" has proven to be a marginal strategy, at best, and has weak biblical support. The ultimate reason teenagers stop following Christ after high school is that *they can*. I mean, they're not "ruined" for him, as Peter was when Jesus asked if he was going to leave, too. A disciple's answer to that question is something like: "I don't understand a lot of what you're saying, and I can't comprehend the things you do, but I know I have nowhere else to go. You've ruined me for you." Disciples answer this way because of the depth of their attachment to Jesus.

Because of the vast number of other environmental forces that are shaping teenagers today, *only* a deeper attachment to Jesus has any chance of stopping the church's slide toward the abyss. But before we move into a deeper exploration of what this means, and what it might look like in your ministry, we must first assess the power of those other environmental forces in teenagers' lives to discover why our current strategies to reach them have little or no hope of succeeding.

CHAPTER TWO

THE INEXORABLE POWER OF ENVIRONMENT

"Christ be with me, Christ within me. Christ behind me, Christ before me. Christ beside me, Christ to win me. Christ to comfort and restore me. Christ beneath me, Christ above me. Christ in quiet, Christ in danger. Christ in hearts of all that love me. Christ in mouth of friend and stranger." —St. Patrick

So if my Batman reference didn't already relegate me to the Dark Ages, I'm sure this obscure reference will remove all doubt: *The Undersea World of Jacques Cousteau*. While *Batman* was my favorite afternoon TV addiction, *The Undersea World* was my favorite nighttime expedition. Cousteau was the beanie-wearing French captain of the Calypso, a floating marine-science laboratory and the real-life setting for a deep-ocean exploration show that seems quaint compared to contemporary reality shows. Like Captain Kirk, his fictional precursor, Captain Cousteau was likewise "boldly going where no man had gone before"—Kirk to the stars, Cousteau to the ocean floor. For a culture that had never really known much about what was happening below the surface of the sea, the deep-ocean environment was a revelation. And Cousteau's job was to translate his passionate curiosity about these mysterious, beautiful, and vaguely dangerous environments to the slack-jawed masses. It was impossible to watch this show and not feel a kind of awe for the way extreme environments shape their inhabitants. Cousteau's cameras revealed a bizarre panoply of species that had acclimated to their dark underworld.

And the way we "acclimate" to our own environments literally forms our identity. The great 20th-century cultural philosopher Marshall McLuhan said: "Environments are not passive wrappings, but are rather active processes which are invisible."[12] We are immersed in the "active processes" of our environments, but we rarely pay attention to their influence on us. For example, what's the lighting like where you are right now? If you're like me, if it's fluorescent lighting you can't wait to get out of there and find a warmer, incandescent environment. I hate the cold, flat light that fluorescents give off, because the impact on my soul is deadening.

When I lead youth workers through an eight-hour experience of Jesus-centered ministry, I ask them to wander around our meeting room for three minutes, taking notes on every aspect of our environment using their five senses and considering how these "background" forces are impacting them emotionally. Then I ask them to go outside the building into a more "natural" environment and do the same thing. When we gather back together, I list all of their environmental forces, and how they impact participants, on a flip chart. We compare the "inside" and "outside" lists, and people are always shocked by how these environmental forces have been influencing their emotional reality.

The Ocean Teenagers Swim In

Even in these innocuous ways, it's amazing how our environments shape us. We simply don't often pay close attention to them because they seem like "passive wrappings" to us. So, what about environmental forces that are obviously non-innocuous? Today's teenage "fish" are swimming in an ocean environment characterized by significant and obvious forces.

- **Margin-less spaces**—More than any other time in human history, we're living in a culture without margin. For those 30 and older, this isn't a native environment. But for everyone else, this is simply called "normal." Every minute of every day, here's what's happening in our margin-less spaces:

  - YouTube users upload 48 hours of new videos;

  - Google receives more than 2 million search queries;

  - Apple receives about 47,000 app downloads;

  - Blog owners on Tumblr put up 27,778 new posts;

  - Flickr users add 3,125 new photos;

  - 571 new websites are created;

  - Instagram users share 3,600 new photos;

  - Twitter users send more than 100,000 tweets;

– Facebook users post 684,478 new pieces of content;

– Emailers send 204,166,667 messages; and

– Consumers spend $272,070 shopping online.[13]

These stats were out-of-date the moment I typed them. The margin, whatever it is, is much thinner at the moment you're reading these words than the moment I typed them. Because we have no buffer zones of temporary boredom in our lives anymore, we're forced to multitask everything, including our relationships.

- **"Flattened" authority in families**—Social researchers who study the buying habits of parents have discovered that collaborative decision-making is now the norm in families. That means most families are no longer top-down enterprises. Collaboration translates to "one person, one vote" environments where influence and leverage, rather than authority, rules. This is one reason why almost all children and teenagers consider their parents as some of their best friends.

- **Normalized "abominations"**—I know, *abomination* is a serious Old Testament word; it means exceptionally loathsome. I came up with "normalized abominations" after listening to an NPR report on the popular teen show *Gossip Girl*. In one episode, three-way sex (a ménage à trois) was treated as a normal rite of passage for incoming college freshmen. This was so out of bounds that the "sleeping giant" in our culture—the collective voice of American parents—got riled up about it. They sent NPR dozens of angry notes about the report. So after the hosts had read a few of the letters, they quickly and seamlessly moved into a request for listeners to offer their ideas for their favorite Thanksgiving traditions. The bizarre and disgusting sat side by side with the warm and inviting, with the effect that "exceptionally loathsome" was normalized by "exceptionally wholesome." I mean, when you place something disgusting next to something that's not, normal spills onto abnormal, making it seem not so bad. Examples of this dynamic in our culture are everywhere.

• **Operational entitlement**—David Walsh, founder of the National Institute on Media and the Family, says the new norm in Western culture is represented by four words: *more, fast, easy, fun.*[14] We're herded like sheep into a cultural "corral" that's defined by the relentless quest for more of everything, the necessity for things to be faster than they were yesterday, the imperative that impediments be cleared from our path, and the assurance that our inalienable right to party will never be threatened. The collective effect of this new norm produces "operational entitlement"— that is, the very structure of our culture insinuates that we deserve more than what we have. This has led to a culture dominated by what teenagers describe as "too-muchness."

- **Worried, fearful, scattered, distracted, overwhelmed, and disconnected parents**—For many years, I've led a two-hour seminar for parents called "Fighting the Entitlement Dragon." The seminars are always packed, because (I've learned) most parents are frustrated and desperate for help in responding to their kids' entrenched attitudes of entitlement. Through the small-group conversations that are part of the seminar, as well as the long conversations I have with parents who line up to talk to me afterward, I've learned a lot about their reality. And these words— worried, fearful, scattered, distracted, overwhelmed, and disconnected—pretty well describe how I've experienced them. What would it be like to grow up in a home led by "active process" parents who live out these words every day?

Jeremy Lin and Popular Theology

Of course, the environmental forces I've listed here hardly make a dent in the vast universe of cultural influences that are boring into your students' lives right now. I usually give youth workers these five kick-starters, then ask them to work together to come up with a more extensive list of forces that are shaping kids today that we condense into one master list. I have to limit the brainstorming to just five minutes, because it would take too long to list everything they come up with. If you set this book down for 30 seconds, you could probably think of at least five additional environmental forces right off the bat (social media? pornography? texting? academic pressures? moral relativism?).

Added on top of these forces, like a cherry on top of our cultural sundae, is something equally influential but harder to pinpoint. It's called popular theology. I mean the kind of pragmatic narrative we tell ourselves about God and religion and spirituality. Popular theology is more *popular* than we realize. God-talk, spiritual conversation, and religious problem-solving are deeply and widely woven into the fabric of our daily lives. But, as with many environmental forces, we're often oblivious to the leverage this sort of "folk theology" has on our own belief systems, let alone the more malleable belief systems of adolescents.

Here's one of my favorite examples of this dynamic, from the liberal-leaning political commentary show *The Young Turks*, hosted by Ana Kasparian and Cenk Uygur. It bills itself as the first-ever live Web-streamed news program. Put yourself in the shoes of an average teenager who's surfing online and stumbles across this three-minute segment on NBA basketball phenom Jeremy Lin. What would you be learning about God and those who follow him from this short exchange?[15]

> **Kasparian:** Jeremy Lin turns out to be very religious, he's a Christian... He was completely disastrous until recently. What's interesting is he says he completely changed his mentality. He says he was a micromanager, he wanted to control everything, he kind of lost sight of what the game was really about. So he took a little time away from basketball and focused on his spirituality. And he realized, "You know what, I'm going to go out there and have fun, and not try to

micromanage, and see how things go." Well it turns out that now he's a pretty great player, because he's not trying to control everything. So, look, do I think religion is something that's magically saving him in basketball? No. But I definitely think that trying to let go, enjoy the game, and not trying to micromanage everything is going to help him with his game. I think that goes for everyone in every field of work.

Uygur: My takeaway from this is that I had no idea that Jeremy Lin was the Tim Tebow of the NBA... *(makes the "Tebowing" pose)*

Kasparian: Except he's not obnoxious about his religion...

Uygur: Well, I guess, every time he scores he's not like JEESSSUUSS! It makes sense, because it isn't about the religion. It's about—I know this from my personal life—if you push too hard, you're not going to get it. There is something to be said for, at some point, letting go. But, also, if you're a believer, this answers a question I always ask: [People] always say things like, "Oh, Jesus saved me" or "Jesus is the reason why." And I always think, "Well, why was Jesus messing with you before?" Is he saying, "Watch this, I'm going to get Jeremy Lin to suck, and then later I'll make him good"? Hey, listen, have at it... I don't have any problem with religion as long as you don't make me try to believe it or you don't try to put it into our government...

Kasparian: I think this is one of the upsides of religion. If you take positive things from it, and you learn positive things from it, it can be great. It can be great for your mental health. I think this is very important for [Lin's] mental health because, believe me, trying to control everything and be a micromanager makes you crazy.

The theological themes embedded in this segment aren't at all foreign to the everyday cultural landscape that's common to most teenagers:

- Religion is a private affair. If you go public, you're assumed to be a wacko.

- Belief in God is valuable as a psychological crutch.

- The worst thing you can do, relative to your beliefs about God, is become "obnoxious" about them.

- If you believe in a God who influences people, your God must be either an addled toddler or a capricious puppeteer.

- Religion is really about what we can get, not what we give.

- Watch out for people who get too specific about their religion. It's fine to talk about God, but talking about Jesus is going over the line.

It might sound silly, given the context, but these kinds of messages—reiterated over and over in the public square—have an immersive impact that forms and informs our latent beliefs, just as salt water forms the biology of sea-dwelling animals.

Set Up for Failure

Now, as you're near the end of this short chapter, would you pause for a moment to get in touch with your *emotional reaction* to this exploration of the environmental forces influencing your students?

Likely, you're feeling a little anxious and maybe even overwhelmed by the forming influences the church is "competing" against. It's sobering when we pay attention, even for a short time, to the powerful messages that are inundating our young people, leveraging how they make sense of life, God, others, and themselves. If we're going to have a shot at gaining a foothold for the gospel in their lives, we'd better come at them with a "shock and awe" strategy that rivets their attention and overshadows these corrupting and forceful influences. So, what is our chosen strategy—our "big stick"? I think it's something like this:

"Convince people to learn and adopt a set of God-principles for better living."

If we honestly examine the content and purpose of the church's conventional message, this "understand and apply" imperative is central to almost everything we say and do. We've reduced ourselves to a defensive posture, pleading with kids to ignore their overwhelming environmental influences and adhere, instead, to our "better principles for better living" message. And when we do, we ignore and even negate the biblical goal of ministry, role-modeled by Jesus on that hillside near Capernaum: "You must eat my body and drink my blood if you want any part of me." The goal of youth ministry is inviting teenagers into intimate relationship with Jesus and then mentoring them into what it means to ABIDE in him. But that goal is juxtaposed with the current heavyweight champion: "understand and apply."

I call this dichotomy between the two approaches "Application vs. Attachment."

And if we continue down the "application" road, the church will lose its voice in the culture. In so many ways, it's already been reduced to a whisper. "Attachment" is the only way forward, and it's also a far more biblically true path. Jesus had little interest in "understand-and-apply" strategics, preferring instead to use botanical, gastronomical, and even sexual metaphors that are shocking in their implications and run counter in every way to popular theology and "proper religion." The biblical call to discipleship, promoted and practiced by Jesus, is nothing like our conventional "try harder to do better" mantra. It's more like a scented love letter from our Beloved, who wants us to come to bed.

The Environmental Impact of Parents

By Mark DeVries

I'm a recovering parent of teenagers—all three are now well into adulthood. As a youth worker who's also a parent, I have no doubt which is the harder (and more important) job. When I conduct parenting seminars, I see desperation on so many faces—enough to know that parents of teenagers are an exhausted lot. Like laboratory animals enduring inconsistent shock therapy, these parents are jumpy, anxious, nervous about the new, latest threat to their children's safety (and thus to their own parental sanity).

As a youth worker, it didn't take me long to realize that I could never build a thriving ministry without partnering with parents. As a parent, it didn't take me long to realize that relying on my own inconsistent parenting skills wasn't the recipe for producing the kind of faith maturity I prayed to see in my own children. I shudder to think where my kids would be today apart from their church. This world literally "dis-integrates" teenagers, forcing them into premature patchwork identities that grow out of disconnected relationships with adults who know nothing of each other (coaches who don't know the pastors who don't know the parents who don't know the teachers who don't know...). The centrifugal force pulling kids away from a convergent center in which they can develop an integrated identity is so powerful that it's perhaps only in a faith community that young people in today's world can complete the identity-formation process.

Our children's identity was formed not out of our parenting ingenuity but as part and parcel of a life surrounded by a convergent community of adults who knew and respected one another. These adults affirmed similar standards, values, and expectations; they modeled a consistent message around which my children's lives could be ordered. From this side of the parenting journey, I realize now that my primary job as a youth worker isn't to be a camp counselor, not simply to build one-on-one relationships with each young person. I realize my primary work is to be an architect, helping to build a constellation of relationships with Christlike adults for every teenager in my program.

One parent told me the experience of parenting teenagers feels like "being a dachshund in deep snow." I can relate. I've learned enough now to know that God never meant for us to do this parenting thing alone, especially parenting teenagers. I shudder to think where my kids would be without their youth ministry.

—*Mark DeVries is President of Youth Ministry Architects and Associate Pastor for Youth and Their Families at First Presbyterian Church, Nashville, Tennessee.*

CHAPTER THREE
THE DISCIPLESHIP FALLACIES

"If you think you can walk in holiness without keeping up perpetual fellowship with Christ, you have made a great mistake. If you would be holy, you must live close to Jesus."
—Charles Haddon Spurgeon

I was invited to have lunch with six youth pastors who'd been singled out by a seminary professor as men and women who'd managed to build long-term, thriving youth ministries. For two hours we talked about the centrality of Jesus as a ministry focus. It wasn't a light conversation; the deeper we dived, the more dissonant the atmosphere became. Finally, one of the youth pastors looked at me with sad-but-determined eyes and said, "I don't think kids walking into our church get to see what it looks like to live as Christians. Most are just there to be with their friends. Our committed Christian kids don't like it—they can't really worship because it's not a worshipful environment. We have attenders but no community."

Another spoke up, obviously feeling the freedom to finally drag into the light what he'd been too afraid to say. "The word *Christian* has taken on alternate meanings in today's culture—we need to throw it out," he said. "We need to debunk how [teenagers] have been brought up to see Jesus, and what worship is all about. If we could just shut down for a year..."

The first speaker jumped in and proclaimed, "I'd love to shut down for a year! Sometimes we're so comforting and so kind and so welcoming we miss the hard edges of Jesus." He went on to describe a conversation he'd had with one of his adult leaders after all the teenagers in that leader's small group quit the group. For more than two years, the youth pastor and the adult leader had worked hard to make the small-group environment safe and welcoming. But the kids finally decided they couldn't stand any more talk about Jesus being the "only way" to salvation.

I asked the other youth pastors at the table to respond to what these two guys were talking about. One tried to probe deeper into the small-group story, clearly skeptical that an entire small group of teenagers would quit only because the leader emphasized Jesus too much. He asked the first speaker if maybe he'd given up too quickly on the group or whether he'd worked hard enough to build a warm relational environment. The first speaker responded that the group had been functioning for two years, and the environment was just as warm and relational as their other small groups.

The group sat in awkward silence for a moment. Their top-of-mind "fixes" didn't resonate, and the dissonance produced by this story was making them uncomfortable.

Then one of them spoke up: "I spent some time this year leading a mission trip overseas. Something happened inside of me during that time. When I came back, I told my kids, 'I'm sick of being a Christian; I'm ready to become a Christ-follower.' For the kids in my church, there's nothing I've ever said that resonated more with them, or longer. These are kids who've grown up in the church, and they want more."

Around our little circle, heads nodded and eyes flashed. These were all highly educated, trench-tested veteran youth pastors who'd each been at their churches for many years and had hundreds of kids in their ministries. They were clearly mature in their faith and admired for their leadership skills. They exhibited no embittered sense of burnout; quite the contrary, actually. I could sense they were all more passionate about youth ministry than ever before. They just didn't like what their ministries had become. And they knew that a few little tweaks or the latest tips and techniques wouldn't get the job done. Half of them were openly hungering to know Jesus more deeply, wishing they could implode their conventional "understand and apply" ministries without losing their job.

It's Not About the Shoulds

It's tempting to simply convince teenagers to leave behind "Christian" and begin anew as "Christ-followers"—but, of course, we can't "should" teenagers into an all-in relationship with Jesus, any more than I "shoulded" my wife into marrying me. For true intimacy to grow in any relationship, we have to be captured and consumed by our lover's *essence*. Pastor and theologian N.T. Wright says: "The longer you look at Jesus, the more you will want to serve him. That is, of course, if it's the real Jesus you're looking at."[16] It's "the real Jesus" whose gravitational pull is so strong that we can't escape his orbit once we get close to him. Philosophy professor and C.S. Lewis scholar Dr. Peter Kreeft once told a class of Boston University students:

"Christ changed every human being he ever met.... If anyone claims to have met him without being changed, he has not met him at all. When you touch him, you touch lightning.... I think Jesus is the only man in history who never bored anyone. I think this is an empirical fact, not just a truth of faith. It's one of the reasons for believing his central claim, and Christianity's central claim, that he is literally God in the flesh.... The Greek word used to describe everyone's reaction to him in the Gospels is 'thauma'— wonder. This was true of his enemies, who killed him. Of his disciples, who worshipped him. And even of agnostics, who went away shaking their heads and muttering 'No man ever spoke like this man' and knowing that if he didn't stop being what he was and saying what he said that eventually they would have to side with either his killers or his worshippers. For 'Jesus shock' breaks your heart in two and forces you to choose which half of your heart you will follow...."[17]

In our conventional understand-and-apply mentality, our central role is to answer kids' questions with something like prophetic wisdom. We're always on the hot seat, and we're always feeling ill-equipped to wow kids with the sort of zinger-answers that C.S. Lewis or G.K. Chesterton or Timothy Keller or Lee Strobel might reel off in the moment. The last time I felt as well-equipped as C.S. Lewis to answer teenagers' unanswerable theological questions was... never.

Urban youth ministry expert Leneita Fix gave me this sampler of questions, asked one night by her small group of senior highers:

> *How do I know if someone is demon-possessed?*

> *Why doesn't my Jewish friend believe Jesus is the Messiah?*

> *Don't Jewish people believe Abraham is Satan?*

> *In those paranormal-type movies, are ghosts and demons the same thing?*

> *Why don't we ever get to stop sinning?*

> *Why does my Jehovah's Witness friend make me feel like I'm the one who's wrong?*

Good luck with those, Leneita. When we accept our "answer-person" job description, we back ourselves into the corner of incapacity sooner or later. All of us will get crammed into that corner because "the right answers" have replaced "the right orientation," and it's literally impossible for any human being to respond well to the myriad environmental forces that are leveraging our teenagers—even the relative few we've already cataloged in the previous chapter. Frustration is a foregone conclusion, *because we don't have all the answers*, and we have a pretty miserable record of teaching people to "apply" truths. Real transformation, even in our own experience, most often happens differently than "understand and apply."

In a Group Magazine survey , we asked Christian college students to look back over their trajectory and identify the factors that caused them to grow and mature as followers of Christ. They told us their primary catalysts included:

1. Parents

2. A crisis or a great struggle

3. A camp or retreat experience

The common thread among these influences is that they're all *identity-forming* forces rather than *understand-and-apply* forces. You'll see this reality threaded through their comments:

- "After my best friend's 7-year-old brother died, I realized the reality of death and heaven and wanted to live my life for Christ."

- "I was at a church camp and was really drawn to God. I had been pretty stagnant and decided to get 'more serious.' "

- "I went to Mexico and experienced what it was to truly serve and know God."

- "When I was about 15, I attended a youth conference, and it kind of woke me up as to getting more serious about my faith. Letting my parents' faith that I grew up with my whole life become my own, so to speak."

- "During a mission trip I realized what an important part God was in my life and how I needed to trust him with my life. I knew I needed to make him the center of my life and the main influence."

It's not that these experiences had no *information* threaded through them, or that the students who said these things weren't encouraged to apply truths to their lives. But the *engine* at the center of these experiences is far more about "who I am" than "what I know." And in contrast to relational experiences that shape our identity in Christ, the understand-and-apply heresy promotes two glaring fallacies:

1. "Understand and apply" assumes that mere understanding leads to growth. If understanding alone were a true indicator of growth as a disciple, then Satan should step to the head of the class. He knew enough biblical truth to go toe-to-toe with Jesus in the wilderness. Understanding alone, it's obvious, does not guarantee transformation. But this assertion nevertheless hangs on with the staying power of a cockroach in a nuclear holocaust. The Enlightenment kicked off a common understanding about rational thought that has become an entrenched *given* in our culture: The most important ingredient in any recipe for growth or maturation is the progression of thought. On one level, that would mean the smartest people are also the most mature, and it takes very little investigative effort to debunk that premise. In fact, you'd be hard-pressed to make the case that Jesus' disciples upended the ancient world because of their advanced understanding of biblical truth. No, they upended the ancient world because they'd been transformed by their intimate relationship with the Spirit of Jesus, now living inside them because of Pentecost.

In his High Priestly Prayer (John 17), Jesus tells his Father out loud that he accomplished everything he'd been given to do. But most of his prayer orbits a profound truth: "It will be better for them when I leave, so I'm going to leave." Why would Jesus be so excited to leave? Well, the road to Emmaus demonstrates that, for at least two of his disciples, much of what the Good Shepherd Jesus tried to get across to his sheep hadn't really "stuck." They'd heard him, lived with him, and watched him, but they hadn't yet been transformed by him. One crucial step was left: to move from an *outside* influence to an *inside* influence. And that's why the Holy Spirit is so necessary. The Spirit makes it possible for us to move from *knowing about* Jesus to *knowing* Jesus. This is *knowing* in the "biblical sense"—it's our most intimate act.

2. "Understand and apply" assumes that our growth in Christ is dependent on our ability, or willingness, to apply truth to our lives. Try this experiment the next time you're listening to a pastor's sermon: Count the number of times some version of "apply this to your life" is mentioned. Then ask yourself: "What's the likelihood that most people sitting in this room will leave here and immediately begin applying these truths to their lives?" Or even more telling: "What's the likelihood that most people in this room even *understand* how to apply the truths they just heard or have the willpower to consider applying them?"

It's tempting for those of us in ministry to gravitate toward judgment when we drill into such questions. We entertain a whispering voice that accuses: "These stupid sheep just don't know what's good for them." And we'd be right, actually. Jesus described the people of God as sheep for good reason. They're not exactly quick of mind, if you know what I mean. The sheep don't need a better understanding of how to avoid getting eaten by wolves; they need a deeper trust in and obedience to their Shepherd, who will look out for them, defend them, and rescue them.

A Radical Rewriting of Our Job Description

In his book *Ruthless Trust*, author Brennan Manning wrote: "It must be noted that Jesus alone reveals who God is.... We cannot deduce anything about Jesus from what we think we know about God; however, we must deduce everything about God from what we know about Jesus."[18] This is so true that it makes me ache inside with longing. The imperative lurking in Manning's blast of truth is an eccentric, ultra-curious, passionate pursuit of everything Jesus said and did. We learn "everything about God" from paying much, much closer attention to Jesus than we ever have before. And when we do, we'll rediscover the original path to a transformed life, laid out by the Trinity from the dawn of time: "Eat my body, drink my blood." This is the summation of all our cliffhangers.

The movement from "mastering knowledge" and growing students' impetus to act on that knowledge, to something that looks and sounds more like a growing romance that "ruins" the lover for the Beloved is at the core of the Jesus-centered ministry shift. And to make this shift, we'll need to do something that couples who've been married a long time and have grown dull to one another's beauty must do: We must remember the Jesus we didn't know we'd forgotten.

A fair reading of the macro narrative of the Bible is this simple condensation: (1) The people of God are rescued by God and live gratefully, for a while; (2) The people of God slowly, inexorably forget what God has done and who he is, and they slide into independence and self-worship; (3) Because of God's great love for his people, God intervenes in their downward slide by releasing the floodgates of consequence for their betrayal; (4) The people of God are jolted awake and remember their desperate need for God; (5) The people of God draw near to God again and rediscover his beauty and strength and truth; (6) The cycle then repeats itself.

Remembering, therefore, is central to God's movement in our lives. That means *forgetting* is our greatest enemy, and there's never a time riper for seducing us into forgetting than when we're pretty comfortable in our understanding of Jesus. And that time is *this time*. We're way, way too comfortable and satisfied in our knowledge and understanding and experience of Jesus. That's why *discomfort* is so closely associated with *remembering*. Pain has the power to blow away the fog produced by our determined commitment to live our lives independent from God; our forgetting is caused by a sense that we have everything under control ourselves. And the more *on top of things* the sheep think they are, the more exposed they are to danger, because they'll be less interested in listening to and obeying their Shepherd and more committed to fighting their own (impossible-to-win) battles.

Paul, in his old age and with the end of his life on the horizon, gave his protégé Timothy this bit of parting advice (emphasis added): "*Remember* Jesus Christ, raised from the dead, descended from David. This is my gospel, for which I am suffering even to the point of being chained like a criminal" (2 Timothy 2:8-9). Paul was imprisoned because of his aggressive pursuit of Jesus, and Timothy had lived through beatings and shipwrecks and imprisonments with him—all for the glory and honor of Jesus. Why would Paul have to *remind* Timothy about Jesus? I think it was because he was humble enough to admit the truth: Everyone, including Paul, Timothy, John the Baptist, Peter, and the disciples... and now you and me... are notorious forgetters.

I was listening to a well-known church consultant talk about cultural trends that are having an impact on the church today. I heard lots of facts and illustrations about "top down" versus "bottom up," "dictatorial" versus "participatory," "isolating" versus "connecting," "big box" versus "intimate space," and so on.

And then my "ruined for Jesus" obsession kicked in.

I realized the church consultant was *only* exploring horizontal strategies—I mean, plans and ideas and techniques that promise to influence the way we help young people experience church and Christian fellowship. To me, it was a very, very interesting discussion about the cup holders in a Ferrari. Who cares about the accessories when you have, sitting under the hood, an engine that can propel the car at speeds above 200 mph? But almost all the very, very interesting discussions and movements in youth ministry are about cup holders—techniques and philosophies and approaches that excite because they're new or edgy or hip. And they're *incredibly boring* when placed side by side with the person of Jesus.

I raised my hand to ask a question: "I'd like to throw out to you my own little 'ax to grind' and get your response. Everything you're talking about is very interesting but very horizontal to me, so where does the pursuit of Jesus fit into all this?"

The church consultant looked at me for an uncomfortably long moment. My question was a dangerous rabbit trail that threatened to hijack the narrative she was trying to weave, and she needed to regain control. "Well, of course, we can't forget the story in all this," she said, finally. "In the midst of changing and adapting our ministries to meet the challenges of a rapidly changing culture, we have to hang on to what we've always known." The consultant continued down this path for a few more minutes and then was clearly ready to move on.

So I raised my hand again and said: "Actually, I don't think it's a good idea at all to 'hang on to what we know.' I think we're now at a place where we're so comfortable with Jesus, so confident of who he is and what he's like, that a lot of 'what we know' is actually *wrong*. We've kind of lost interest in him, like a married couple in midlife. We think we pretty much have him pegged—all the things we like and all the things that have been bugging us about him for years. We've been married a long time to Jesus and have gone through a lot together. But one of the marriage partners—the church—is sort of looking around for something to spark our passions because we're past the 'passionate curiosity' stage with Jesus. So we turn to the 'form and function' of doing church as our midmarriage splurge—like letting ourselves get involved in an emotional affair to rouse us from our relational boredom. If we're not awake to this dynamic, our 'marriage' could descend into deadness and a sense of growing isolation. We'll literally live under the same roof with Jesus but live separate lives, functionally apart from him."

When I was finished fire-hosing the consultant with this onslaught, I couldn't tell whether she was arrested by it or merely exercising superhuman patience until I ran out of gas. She nodded, acknowledged my input, and suggested we take a short break. I got up to stretch, and several people quickly surrounded me. Their eyes were flashing with a kind of rebel glee. One said, "What all people—young and old—are *really* hungry for today is Jesus." Our faces lit up, and we felt an immediate and kindred closeness with each other. The excitement of that shared connection was, simply, a nonmusical expression of worship.

And, by the way, that offhand comment about what we're really hungry for is also a fact of research. When Group

Magazine asked more than 25,000 Christian teenagers what topic they were most interested in talking about with their youth leader or other adult ministry leader, their top response was this: "Getting a better understanding of what Jesus really said and did, and how faith in him matters in my own life."

Soapbox Derby Car or Ferrari?

The simple reason a few mostly uneducated and often clueless first-century men and women could plant something that not only changed the world but continues to occupy its orbital center is because their "movement" was attached to the present force of the person of Jesus. They were not the greatest tips-and-techniques people who ever walked the earth. They were not skilled at strategy or structure. But they were ruined for Jesus, and the momentum of that attachment changed everything they touched. In his book *Who Is This Man?* author and pastor John Ortberg sums it up well: "Normally when someone dies, their impact on the world immediately begins to recede. But... Jesus' impact was greater a hundred years after his death than during his life; it was greater still after five hundred years; after a thousand years his legacy laid the foundation for much of Europe; after two thousand years he has more followers in more places than ever.... Jesus' vision of life continues to haunt and challenge humanity. His influence has swept over history like the tail of a comet, bringing his inspiration to influence art, science, government, medicine, and education; he has taught humans about dignity, compassion, forgiveness, and hope."[19]

In our conventional approaches to ministry, we're like little children building a Soapbox Derby car out of plywood for a Formula One race when there's a perfectly good Ferrari sitting there. God isn't expecting us to build our own car out of scrapwood and ingenuity and give it a good push. He's inviting us to sink into the bucket seats of his Ferrari, whose name is Jesus, and open up the throttle...

Entering In With Jesus
By Chap Clark

Sarah began with, "I've never told anybody about this...."
She eventually got to: "You mean Jesus sees who I am and
what I've done? If that's right, then he'd want nothing to do
with me!" In between, Sarah shared with me the long-buried
story of a small child being repeatedly molested by a neighbor.
Sarah had shoved aside shame, guilt, and pain for more than
a decade. She'd tried to pretend she could "handle it" and
yet could never quite shake the feeling that she was a dirty,
unlovable person. It wasn't until that day at camp when Sarah
allowed me into her story that the depths of her anguish
began to spill out.

As we talked, she slowly allowed the wonder of grace to seep
into her soul. For the first time in her life, she began to trust
that Jesus actually cared and, more importantly, could do
something to bring healing to her shredded heart. Sarah's
story is unique, but only in its particulars. One of the major
shifts that's taken place in youth ministry the last few years
is that stories eerily similar to Sarah's are becoming more
commonplace. The issue may not be sexual, although far
more of our kids than we realize are victims of some form
of sexual abuse. But almost every teenager is sheltering a
hidden past or harrowing present that causes them deep pain.
The amazing thing is that in youth ministry we remain so
committed to getting kids to "come" and to "accept" Christ (a
term, incidentally, that's not even in the Bible) that we don't
do a very good job at communicating the good news that God
accepts them already, brokenness and all.

As we represent Jesus Christ to students in youth ministry, our call is to follow him in how he approached, honored, and cared for those he longed to redeem. In John 4 we're told that Jesus broke the law, at least the law of social convention, when he sat alone with a "Samaritan-gone-wild" woman at a lonely well. He had sent his disciples into town ostensibly to buy food, but from the context it appears that Jesus knew exactly what he had in mind as he approached the well.

Although the details are obscure at best, the way that Jesus engaged this lonely, outcast woman is astounding. First, he connected with her by initiating a relationship. The woman certainly would have minded her own business if Jesus hadn't broken in. But then he moves from connecting to honoring her by how he not only continued the conversation but deepened it. She wasn't a "ministry target"—his treatment of her demonstrated that he saw her as a precious daughter of his Father. As Jesus drew her into a real relationship by talking with her, he let her know she mattered to him.

After Jesus had established a connection and then honored her with the gift of conversation, he entered her story. In the text this turn looks rather abrupt, but a careful read reveals that there had to be more to the encounter. When the time was right and trust had been established, Jesus invited himself into her world by asking a probing question. Her response makes it clear that the way he connected, honored, and eventually came alongside her story was a little frightening to her, but she nevertheless experienced a rare and welcome emotional embrace. As they talked, he then drew her into his story, the story of redemption.

This is what we do. Jesus-centered youth ministry means we are initiators, committed friends, and gentle counselors who, like Jesus, don't push. Rather, we're present, available, and on the lookout for the opportunity to care. Like Jesus, this means at our core we're committed to building a ministry that

- initiates and connects,

- honors in relationship,

- gently enters the stories of teenagers, and

- always points to the great Healer, Jesus.

—*Chap Clark is a Professor of Youth, Family, and Culture at Fuller Theological Seminary and Senior Editor of Youthworker Journal.*

CHAPTER FOUR
JESUS AND HIS BOTANICAL BENT

"Christ changed every human being he ever met.... If anyone claims to have met him without being changed, he has not met him at all. When you touch him, you touch lightning."
—Dr. Peter Kreeft

Let's say you're a foreign-exchange student from India who's been placed in the home of a typical middle-American family. Your English is strong enough to overcome most of the expected language barriers, but some aspects of your "normal life" back home are hard for your host family to understand. The customs of your "foreign culture" don't make much sense to your host family, who haven't been formed by the environmental forces that have saturated your life.

For example, why is it customary to bow instead of shake hands in many Asian cultures? Well, throughout India's history, a jug and the left palm have taken the place of toilet paper, while in Indonesia, one might grow a long fingernail on the left hand for the same purpose. Bowing rather than shaking hands makes perfect sense in the context of these pragmatic differences, and a necessary practice morphed into a custom over time. These customs are hard to fathom for people who are divorced from the context that created them. If you're that foreign-exchange student, you'll need help not only overcoming the language barrier but translating your homeland's customs and norms.

And the normal practices of the "foreign culture" of the kingdom of God require a similar translation. Remember, original sin kicked us out of the Garden, our original home with God. We were exiled "east of Eden," forcibly transferred from the kingdom of God to the "kingdom of this earth." And now we've sojourned so long in this unfamiliar land that we have no inherent understanding of the customs and practices of God's native home. So Jesus must translate these realities into something we can understand—something that gives us a flavor of the mystery that is his personality and kingdom. So he uses metaphors and parables to help bridge the gap of understanding—to use what we know in our context to help us understand what's foreign to us about his homeland: "The disciples came to him and asked, 'Why do you speak to the people in parables?' He replied, 'The knowledge of the secrets of the kingdom of heaven has been given to you, but not to them. Whoever has will be given more, and he will have an abundance. Whoever does not have, even what he has will be taken from him. This is why I speak to them in parables: "Though seeing, they do not see; though hearing, they do not hear or understand" ' " (Matthew 13:10-13).

Jesus is "planting" metaphors and parables, like seeds, so that insights into God's character and kingdom slowly grow in us. Maybe those seeds stay in the soil of our souls until they're watered and fertilized, then poke through into the light of our understanding. We all need the special help of metaphors and parables to understand a God who is more glorious and beautiful than our natural understanding or our fallen human context can comprehend. And what happens when we more deeply understand the values and priorities of the kingdom of God? In Matthew 13:52, Jesus says: "Every teacher of the law who has been instructed about the kingdom of heaven is like the owner of a house who brings out of his storeroom new treasures as well as old." When you have embraced and adopted the "cultural norms" of the kingdom of God, you can give others the treasures they need, whenever they need them. You're like a generous, well-stocked store. Our kingdom-of-God purpose is to give "out of our good treasure"—but we have no treasure to give unless we follow the path laid out by Jesus' metaphors. And his favorite genre of metaphor is botanical.

Dying Branches and the Living Vine

Recently I hid clues to a mystery-person's identity all around a meeting area. Twenty minutes into my presentation, I told the crowd of youth pastors what I'd done. I described the mystery person as someone they all knew or have heard about. Their job was to find as many clues as they could in 60 seconds, then get together with a few others to share their clues and make their best guess as to who the mystery person was. After a few groups offered the wrong answer, one correctly guessed SpongeBob SquarePants. Then I told them that these clues had been hiding there, all around them, but they never would've noticed them if I hadn't challenged them to pay attention and search. And I told them this little scavenger hunt is a picture of a kingdom-of-God reality.

God has done something similar in our world; he's hidden clues to who he really is, and what he's really like, all around us. But we have to pay attention to "get" them. Paul, in Romans 1:20 (NASB), says: "Since the creation of the world His invisible attributes, His eternal power and divine nature, have been clearly seen, being understood through what has been made." God believes so strongly in the power of metaphor that he's actually planted his story in everything he's created, not just in the stories and teachings of Jesus. He's embedded clues to the kingdom of God throughout the created world in an attempt to show us who he is and what he does. That's why there are 8.74 million species in the world—and almost half a million (400,000) are plants. Thousands of new species are discovered every year. Researchers estimate it will still take hundreds of years for human beings, with all our clever little gadgets and unsatiated curiosity, to discover them all.

Why all this "useless beauty," to quote Elvis Costello? Why such extravagant variety? Because God's "love language" is metaphor. Our everyday world is teeming with them. And Jesus defined discipleship and growth using metaphors, most often in botanical terms: "I am the Vine, you are the branches. When you're joined with me and I with you, the relation intimate and organic, the harvest is sure to be abundant. Separated, you can't produce a thing. Anyone who separates from me is deadwood, gathered up and thrown on the bonfire" (John 15:5-6, THE MESSAGE). Later, Paul builds on the foundation of Jesus' metaphor by extending its meaning: "If some of the branches have been broken off, and you, though a wild olive shoot, have been grafted in among the others and now share in the nourishing sap from the olive root, do not boast over those branches. If you do, consider this: You do not support the root, but the root supports you" (Romans 11:17-18).

This grafted-into-the-Vine metaphor is telling us a kingdom-of-God truth—that we're dying branches in desperate need of attaching ourselves to a growing Vine, and the Vine is Jesus himself. The truth is that transformation happens when we draw near to Jesus, because he's the only One who can really change us. "Original sin" breaks off our "branch" from fellowship with God, from his family. In our fallen state we are attached, really, to the family of Satan (that's why Jesus tells the Pharisees they are "of your father, Satan"). When we repent, we break away from that toxic vine and attach ourselves to the Living Vine. My friend Ned Erickson once shared with me something he calls "The Progression." It goes like this: "Get to know Jesus well, because the more you know him, the more you'll love him, and the more you love him, the more you'll want to follow him, and the more you follow him, the more you'll become like him, and the more you become like him, the more you become yourself."[20] A "self" that is fully alive, and fully itself, is the organic outcome of a deepening attachment to the Vine. And it's the organic outcome that Jesus is after, not "try harder to get better."

If you're not an avid gardener, you likely have no idea how the process of grafting actually works. I know I didn't. So I decided to find out. My wife and I visited a local nursery and asked a Master Gardener to explain grafting to us. Fifteen minutes later, we were in tears as the reality of this metaphor barreled into our souls.

- First you need a hardy "rootstock"—a plant that's vigorous and full of life and energy.

- When you're grafting, you typically choose a weaker, less hardy plant to graft into the stronger, acclimated root.

- Professionals typically use grafting only when they want to make a hybrid plant—"a new creature"— something that can live and thrive in a particular climate with stronger roots than its natural ones.

- Grafting is an art; it's not easy to make a graft work. You have to know what you're doing and exercise patience. If you do it badly or quickly or haphazardly, the graft won't take.

- When you're ready to graft, you cut a branch from a weaker, low-producing tree.

- The leaves from the weaker branch are then cut off, leaving only nubs.

- The end of the weaker branch is whittled into a point, and the rootstock of the stronger tree is cut down the middle, leaving it open for the grafted branch to "seat" in the cut.

- Then the grafted branch is fit into the cut on the stronger tree, and the graft is wrapped with tape to keep it joined. It's an intimate bonding.

- Finally, over time, the life of the grafted branch becomes part of the life of the strong tree. Its life is derived entirely from the root, hidden in it, part of a new species. The tape can be removed, and the grafted tree is moved outside so it can be exposed to the elements and "harden."

This botanical metaphor for our life with Jesus is a description of a kind of intimacy that's so consuming it seems almost improper to talk about it at church. It's why we let this statement by Jesus roll off our tongues—"I am the Bridegroom, you are my bride"—with little recognition of the raw intimacy he's describing. It's the same raw intimacy represented by "I am the vine, you are my [grafted] branches."

After I'd experienced the metaphor of grafting for myself, I started searching for a way to let others taste its depth. I found a short demonstration of grafting on YouTube—two Master Gardeners from Australia showing exactly how to graft a branch from a weak and low-producing fruit tree into a strong and vigorous one. You can find it by simply typing "grafting fruit trees" into the search box on YouTube, then scrolling to find the video titled exactly that way. Or simply go here: youtube.com/watch?v=-EwtyO16dFg. I've now shown this three-minute video to thousands of youth workers, then asked them to tell me what they saw in this metaphor that's true about our relationship with Jesus. I write everything they say on big flipcharts, and when we're finished the room is always baptized by tears:

- Sin tore us away from our true Father and grafted us into a family of rebellion, a family infected with sin.

- Jesus told us he didn't come to bring peace but a sword—a sword that would cut us away from our rebellious family, the only family we've ever known. The pain we experience in life—the cuts that wound— actually make it possible for our grafting to happen. This is why, after Paul pleads with Jesus to take away the "messenger of Satan sent to buffet me," Jesus tells him this: "My grace is sufficient for you, for my power is made perfect in weakness" (2 Corinthians 12:9).

- Remember, Jesus said we are the branches and he is the Vine. It takes an "open wound" on both the branch and the vine to complete the graft. Our wounds open us to Jesus, and his wound was inflicted on the cross. Once during this grafting debrief, someone offered this insight: "I know the exact moment when the knife sliced into Jesus' soul. When he cried out on the cross, 'My God, My God, why have you forsaken me?'"

- The bond is intimate but not instantaneous; it requires a lot of time for the graft to "take."

- The life in our "dying branch" is slowly ebbing away.

You can feel it happen when you cut a leafy branch from a tree and the leaves slowly lose their firmness. Birth is the beginning of the end for us. A death is working in us that's common to all human beings. We need a rescue from this death, the kind that only a Living Vine can offer us.

- Over time, the life of the root enters into the grafted branch. The whole thing becomes a new thing. Our good and true and beautiful Father found a way to graft us back in to himself, to generously offer us his life, his truth, his intimacy.

- Jesus is telling us that our true Father wants to graft us back into his very own family, where we will one day occupy one of the "many rooms in my Father's house" that Jesus spoke about as he prepared his disciples for the horror of the cross.

Get closer to Jesus by attaching yourself to him and you'll find life, and the life will literally transform you, and your transformation will produce fruit, which will look a lot like the fruit of the Spirit, the same stuff we've been told to "apply to our life." In the popular understand-and-apply version of discipleship that's propagated in the church, we're told to grab what fruit we can and sort of duct-tape it to our soul. In the Vine-and-branch version, we produce fruit because of Who we're attached to.

The Smell of Jesus

I started out a training time with some national youth ministry leaders by asking them to get with a partner. Then I gave each pair a brown bag with the same hidden object inside. I gave one person in each pair, the Teacher, permission to reach into the bag and touch the object for just 30 seconds. Then the Teacher had to describe it to his or her partner, the Learner. I told the Teachers they couldn't use the object's name to describe it.

Afterward, I asked the Learners, "What is the object?" No one guessed correctly. Then I asked the Teachers, "What is the object?" Some knew what it was but couldn't describe it well enough for their partner to guess it. Others had no idea what the object was, even after handling it in the bag for 30 seconds. Then I asked them to pull the object out of their bags. It was a little Gumby-like bendable man. After the laughter died down, I said, "Let's say our little bendy guy represents Jesus. How were the challenges in this activity like the challenges we face in teaching today's kids about Jesus?"

After some uncomfortable silence, one guy spoke up and said something like: "The biggest challenge is knowing Jesus intimately enough to describe him to others, and we have a lot going on that's keeping us from knowing him intimately." Amen. If Jesus walked into the room, would we recognize the sound of his voice? that look in his eyes? his unmistakable "otherness"? Would we know him so intimately that we could recognize his smell?

Our own growing attachment to Jesus fuels our continued pursuit of him. Leadership in youth ministry is really about extending the momentum of our intimate connection to Jesus into ever-widening circles. One youth pastor who's shifted his ministry's focus to a Jesus-centered approach told me: "Everything's birthed out of listening. You're growing, so you pass what's happening in you on to the kids in the ministry. [Listening] creates quiet in your heart, and in the quiet everything points back to Jesus."

This leader's comments mesh well with what researchers with the *Exemplary Youth Ministries* study[21] heard when they interviewed pastors, youth pastors, volunteers, and teenagers at each of 21 churches that had been identified as particularly effective in helping students grow deep in their faith. Researchers found a shared singular-passion for the pursuit of Jesus running through the leaders of these ministries. For example, the Rev. Dave Byrum, senior pastor at First United Methodist Church in Valparaiso, Indiana, says: "We put prayer and spiritual formation first with youth. I don't think the cultural expectations of pingpong and a good time are as necessary as the culture thinks it is. We acknowledge that kids are deeply spiritual people and want to be. They're hungry... We still have fun and play wacky games and pingpong and share lots of food, but they're more of a byproduct than the centerpiece." And an adult volunteer at New Colony Baptist Church in Billerica, Massachusetts, says: "It's Jesus. In all honesty, that's the way I see it. We all spend time in prayer. If we didn't, I don't know what would be going on."

This *leaning into* the pursuit of Jesus—where we look for him and listen to him and follow his nudges into all sorts of adventures—is really at the core of a shift to a Jesus-centered youth ministry. It's a movement from "mastery of knowledge and discipline" to a "growing abandonment to the person of Jesus." Paul, in his letter to the Christians in Philippi, declares, "We're waiting the arrival of the Savior, the Master, Jesus Christ, who will... make us beautiful and whole with the same powerful skill by which he is putting everything as it should be, under and around him" (Philippians 3:20-21, THE MESSAGE). We need transformation, not incremental improvement. Understand-and-apply is a me-centered, exhausting, and ultimately demoralizing exercise in manufactured grace. It's the same exercise once practiced by the Pharisees, who Jesus lambasted over and over for practicing a "form of religion" without its "substance"—for caring more about rule-keeping than relationship. We cling to this way of influencing growth because we are controlling. We understand how to do-and-do-and-do, but we don't understand how to abide.

In the Oscar-winning film *Good Will Hunting,* the difference between *mere understanding* and *abiding* is perfectly portrayed in the story of a troubled young genius named Will Hunting. As he moves through life, Will relates to the people around him with rage and cocksure arrogance. He leaves a trail of wrecked relationships and grief in his wake. He's a walking illustration of a psychological truism: "Hurt people hurt people." Will's quick wit and pseudo-intellectual arguments create a kind of magnetism that he leverages to brutalize and betray everyone who tries to get close to him. All of that changes when he's forced to meet with a psychologist named Sean Maguire, a broken man whose wife has recently died after a long battle with cancer. After a particularly disturbing interchange, when Will disparages the psychologist's dead wife, the two meet for their next session at a park bench. Sean, played by Robin Williams, lowers the boom on Will, played by Matt Damon:

SEAN: Thought about what you said to me the other day.... Stayed up half the night thinking about it. Something occurred to me... fell into a deep peaceful sleep, and haven't thought about you since. Do you know what occurred to me?

WILL: No.

SEAN: You're just a boy. You don't have the faintest idea what you're talking about.

WILL: Why, thank you.

SEAN: It's all right. You've never been out of Boston.

WILL: No.

SEAN: So if I asked you about art you could give me the skinny on every art book ever written. Michelangelo, you know a lot about him. Life's work, political aspirations... the whole works, right? But I'll bet you can't tell me what it smells like in the Sistine Chapel. You've never actually stood there and looked up at that beautiful ceiling. If I ask you about women, you'd probably give me a syllabus about your personal favorites.... But you can't tell me what it feels like to wake up next to a woman and feel truly happy.... And I'd ask you about war, you'd probably throw Shakespeare at me, right? "Once more unto the breach, dear friends." But you've never been near one. You've never held your best friend's head in your lap, watch him gasp his last breath looking to you for help. I'd ask you about love; you'd probably quote me a sonnet. But you've never looked at a woman and been totally vulnerable. Known someone that could level you with her eyes, feeling like God put an angel on earth just for you... And you wouldn't know what it's like to be her angel, to have that love for her, be there forever, through anything, through cancer. And you wouldn't know about sleeping sitting up in the hospital room for two months, holding her hand, because the doctors could see in your eyes that the terms "visiting hours" don't apply to you. You don't know about real loss, 'cause it only occurs when you've loved something more than you love yourself. And I doubt you've ever dared to love anybody that much.[22]

Will has understood true things, and he's applied true things, but he isn't *attached* to true things. He's living out of the shell of his identity but doesn't know it until an aging, broken man lowers the boom on his poser life and invites him to move toward the truth. When we emphasize application over attachment in ministry, we risk creating posers who may intellectually embrace things that are true but have never ingested them in their deepest places. The more teenagers understand that Jesus is *our pivot*—that a life with him is so real and intimate that it spills over into every conversation, every activity, every service opportunity, every laughter-filled outing, and every late-night phone call—the more they'll be magnetically drawn to the Jesus you and I are so obviously captivated by. The whole point of the Incarnation—God become man, living among us—is that we now have a path into knowing the heart and soul of our Creator. And that path's name is Jesus, who describes himself as "the Way, the Truth, and the Life."

The picture that comes closest to capturing a Jesus-centered shift in ministry is described in Luke 24:13-32 (NASB), when a pair of disciples traveling the road to Emmaus run into the resurrected Jesus but don't recognize him at first:

> "And behold, two of them were going that very day to a village named Emmaus, which was about seven miles from Jerusalem. And they were talking with each other about all these things which had taken place. While they were talking and discussing, Jesus Himself approached and *began* traveling with them. But their eyes were prevented from recognizing Him. And He said to them, 'What are these words that you are exchanging with one another as you are walking?'

And they stood still, looking sad. One *of them*, named Cleopas, answered and said to Him, 'Are You the only one visiting Jerusalem and unaware of the things which have happened here in these days?' And He said to them, 'What things?' And they said to Him, 'The things about Jesus the Nazarene, who was a prophet mighty in deed and word in the sight of God and all the people, and how the chief priests and our rulers delivered Him to the sentence of death, and crucified Him. But we were hoping that it was He who was going to redeem Israel. Indeed, besides all this, it is the third day since these things happened. But also some women among us amazed us. When they were at the tomb early in the morning, and did not find His body, they came, saying that they had also seen a vision of angels who said that He was alive. Some of those who were with us went to the tomb and found it just exactly as the women also had said; but Him they did not see.' And He said to them, 'O foolish men and slow of heart to believe in all that the prophets have spoken! Was it not necessary for the Christ to suffer these things and to enter into His glory?' Then beginning with Moses and with all the prophets, He explained to them the things concerning Himself in all the Scriptures. And they approached the village where they were going, and He acted as though He were going farther. But they urged Him, saying, 'Stay with us, for it is *getting* toward evening, and the day is now nearly over.' So He went in to stay with them. When He had reclined *at the table* with them, He took the bread and blessed *it*, and breaking *it*, He *began* giving *it* to them. Then their eyes were opened and they recognized Him; and He vanished from their sight. They said to one another, 'Were not our hearts burning within us while He was speaking to us on the road, while He was explaining the Scriptures to us?' "

Here Jesus is pursuing the men, asking questions, listening, speaking prophetically about himself, and narrowing their focus to his invitation into intimacy. Though these disciples had known Jesus, they didn't *know* him. They, like Job before them, hadn't crossed over from friendship with God to romantic intimacy with him: "I have declared that which I did not understand, things too wonderful for me, which I did not know. 'Hear, now, and I will speak; I will ask You, and You instruct me.' I have heard of You by the hearing of the ear; but now my eye sees You" (Job 42:3-5, NASB). When we move from a ministry focus that emphasizes "the hearing of the ear" to an environment that helps students experience Jesus, and thus proclaim "now my eye sees You," we are helping their graft to "take." And once they are grafted to Jesus, their identity is caught up in him. They, like Peter, will move into their lives as true disciples who answer, "Where else would I go?" when they're offered the chance to leave him. And fruit will fill up their lives, offering others the nourishment they so desperately need.

Though this shift to a Jesus-centered passion and approach sounds big—and it is—the steps onto this path are remarkably simple. I don't mean this will be like flipping on a light switch; I mean that our ministry focus (which is most often pulled in a thousand directions because we're trying to confront the environmental forces at work in students' lives with an understand-and-apply strategy) can now be reduced to pursuing the answers to two simple questions:

1. Who do I say Jesus is?

2. Who does Jesus say I am?

CHAPTER FIVE

ANSWERING THE ONLY TWO QUESTIONS THAT MATTER

"We are called to an everlasting preoccupation with God... Man was made to worship God... Why did Christ come? In order that He might make worshipers out of rebels. We were created to worship. Worship is the normal employment of moral beings. Worship is a moral imperative. Worship is the missing jewel in modern evangelicalism." —A.W. Tozer

My introduction to the "The Prince of Preachers," 19th-century British pastor and theologian C.H. Spurgeon, was a mustard-seed moment for me—a tiny thing that blew up into an enormous thing. During a break at a gathering for ministry leaders, I was alone in a conference room with my friend Greg Stier, founder and president of Dare 2 Share Ministries. I shared with him the moment I heard Jesus tell me: "You're bored by everything but me now." As Greg listened to my story, his eyes flashed and he sat forward in his chair. Leaning in, he said: "Well, you know, Spurgeon said that no matter what Bible text he was preaching on or what issue he was teaching about, he always made a beeline to the cross—to Jesus."

OK, I thought, *who's Spurgeon and what's a beeline?* I knew next to nothing about the man, although I later learned he'd once been one of the most widely recognized people in the world. And though I'd heard the word *beeline* before, it was eccentric, even quaint, lingo to me.

I asked Greg to tell me about Spurgeon, one of his longtime heroes of the faith. That little taste tantalized me, so I plunged into learning everything I could about Spurgeon and his "beeline" passion. He was born in England and committed his life to Christ in 1850, when he was 15 years old. He preached his first sermon a year later and took on the pastorate of a small Baptist church a year after that, at 17. Just five years after his conversion, the 20-year-old Spurgeon became pastor of London's famed New Park Street Chapel. A few months into his new position, his skill and power as a preacher made him famous—at 22 he was, by far, the most popular religious figure of the day. He preached twice every Sunday, with 6,000 people crowding into both services (before the invention of the microphone). But amid his pervasive fame and influence, Spurgeon was suffering from a birth defect that saddled him with nagging and sometimes-debilitating pain. As a result, he battled depression, on and off, his whole life. At the time, he had more books in print than any other living person. He still has more books in print than any pastor in history, including more than 2,500 of his published sermons.

Spurgeon's determination to "beeline" everything in his life and ministry to Jesus is highlighted in the way he coached beginner pastors in their preaching. Young pastors often invited him to listen to them preach, then give his constructive critique. After one young man's impassioned sermon, Spurgeon delivered his summation. He thought it was well-prepared and well-delivered, but it nevertheless... stunk.

"Will you tell me why you think it a poor sermon?" asked the young pastor.

"Because," said Spurgeon, "there was no Christ in it."

The young man said, "Well, Christ was not in the text; we are not to be preaching Christ always, we must preach what is in the text."

The old man responded, "Don't you know, young man, that from every town, and every village, and every little hamlet in England, wherever it may be, there is a road to London?"

"Yes," said the young man.

"Ah!" said the old preacher, "and so from *every text* in Scripture there is a road to the metropolis of the Scriptures, that is Christ. Dear brother, when you get to a text, say, 'Now, what is the road to Christ?' and then preach a sermon, running along the road towards the great metropolis—Christ."[23]

This is what Spurgeon called "making a beeline to Christ." It was his central, guiding commitment every time he began to speak or teach or write. He wrote: "Jesus is The Truth. We believe in Him—not merely in His words. He is the Doctor and the Doctrine, the Revealer and the Revelation, the Illuminator and the Light of Men. He is exalted in every word of truth, because he is its sum and substance. He sits above the gospel, like a prince on his own throne. Doctrine is most precious when we see it distilling from his lips and embodied in his person. Sermons are valuable in proportion as they speak of him and point to him. A Christless gospel is no gospel at all and a Christless discourse is the cause of merriment to devils."[24]

Spurgeon's passion for Jesus, and his determination to track everything he said and did back to "the metropolis of Christ," is really the central—but often unpursued—imperative in ministry today. That beeline path is boundaried on either side by two questions that are embedded in a remarkable conversation between Jesus and his disciples as they road-tripped through Caesarea Philippi:

1. "Who do I say Jesus is?"

After another tough encounter with the conniving Pharisees, followed by another head-scratching conversation with his confused and clueless disciples, Jesus does something that is shocking for its humility. Matthew, the former tax collector on the take, offers this eyewitness account: "Now when Jesus came into the district of Caesarea Philippi, He was asking His disciples, 'Who do people say that the Son of Man is?' And they said, 'Some *say* John the Baptist; and others, Elijah; but still others, Jeremiah, or one of the prophets.' He said to them, 'But who do you say that I am?' Simon Peter answered, 'You are the Christ, the Son of the living God' " (Matthew 16:13-15, NASB).

2. "Who does Jesus say I am?"

Of course, Peter steps up and answers Jesus with magnificent chutzpah. He, more than any other, is attached to Jesus. But attachment is a two-way street; we name Jesus, and Jesus names us. So Jesus fires back with his own chutzpah: "You are Peter, and upon this rock I will build My church; and the gates of Hades will not overpower it. I will give you the keys of the kingdom of heaven; and whatever you bind on earth shall have been bound in heaven, and whatever you loose on earth shall have been loosed in heaven" (Matthew 16:18-19, NASB).

We name, and are named ourselves, as we beeline our life to Jesus. Our purpose in life narrows in focus, simply, to feeding our fascination of everything he said or did, then moving through life responding to his Spirit's nudges and imperatives. We move Jesus from the background of our everyday activities into the foreground. In an interview with Dr. Christian Smith, I asked him to pinpoint something we should pay particular attention to in the *National Study of Youth and Religion*. Here's what he said:

> "Even though most teens are very positive about religion and say it's a good thing, the vast majority are incredibly inarticulate about religion. They could not explain what they believed—hardly at all. They had extreme difficulty in explaining how it affected their lives, other than to say it makes them happy, helps them have a better day, and helps them make some good moral decisions. It seems like religion operates

in the background—it's just part of the wallpaper, part of the furniture. That's important for a couple different reasons. It doesn't seem to us that many teens are being very well-educated in their faith traditions. They aren't being taught how to think and talk about what they believe and how it affects their lives. This is probably the same with parents."[25]

If Jesus, and the way we relate to him, is merely "part of the furniture" of our life, then it's not possible to live out of a replenishing stream of his mission and purpose. We are released into our name (our beautiful and unique and desperately needed strength) when we attach ourselves to Jesus so deeply that we can stand and name him when it costs us to do it. And when we orbit everything we do in ministry around answering these two great questions—"Who do I say Jesus is?" and "Who does Jesus say I am?"—we create a kind of *gravitational pull* that magnetically draws (or sometimes repels) students and adults.

Jesus *does* have a smell, and the closer we get to him the more we smell like him. And, surprisingly, the smell of Jesus is like fresh-baked bread to some and like freshly deposited dung to others: "For we are a fragrance of Christ to God among those who are being saved and among those who are perishing; to the one an aroma from death to death, to the other an aroma from life to life" (2 Corinthians 2:15-16, NASB). This smell— "life to life" or "death to death"—is the stink we want students to wallow in (the Axe of the teenage Christian life).

In fact, I believe "Who do you say Jesus is?" is the *only question* we really need for discipling teenagers. It's such a rich, lifelong, flexible, and satisfying question. We can pursue its mysteries for the rest of our lives and never get tired of the adventure. And as we pursue this question, all other questions can fit under its umbrella. It's Spurgeon's "all roads lead to London" philosophy, and it means that no matter what topic or activity we're exploring, we can find our way to Jesus in a natural, unforced way. "Beelining to Jesus" is like riding a bike. At first we feel awkward and unsteady, and the whole thing seems ridiculous. But then we have stretches when it feels natural, and pretty soon we're exhilarated by the freedom of it, and we forget all about the awkwardness of our first attempts.

Jesus himself practiced "beelining." In John 6:30-33 (THE MESSAGE) some who are part of the growing multitude, drawn to Jesus because of his electrifying miracles, are angling for more of his "supernatural provision." One says: "Moses fed our ancestors with bread in the desert. It says so in the Scriptures: 'He gave them bread from heaven to eat.' " But then Jesus takes the momentum of this man's pursuit and redirects it to himself: "The real significance of that Scripture is not that Moses gave you bread from heaven but that my Father is right now offering you bread from heaven, the *real* bread. The Bread of God came down out of heaven and is giving life to the world." This encounter is an echo of Jesus' conversation with the "woman at the well" outside of Sychar, in John 4. After she misconstrues what he's offering her (she thinks he intends to draw water from the well for her), Jesus tells her the water from Jacob's well is nothing compared to the "living water" of himself. The real thirst-quencher is standing right in front of her. All roads lead to Jesus, even for Jesus.

Who Do I Say Jesus Is?

Jesus was always and everywhere immersing his disciples in the beelined way of life. Here, he nudges Thomas and Philip further onto the path (John 14:4-9): " 'You know the way to the place where I am going.' Thomas said to him, 'Lord, we don't know where you are going, so how can we know the way?' Jesus answered, 'I am the way and the truth and the life. No one comes to the Father except through me. If you really knew me, you would know my Father as well. From now on, you do know him and have seen him.' Philip said, 'Lord, show us the Father and that will be enough for us.' Jesus answered: 'Don't you know me, Philip, even after I have been among you such a long time? Anyone who has seen me has seen the Father.' "

Here, it's good to sink into Jesus' "Don't you know me?" The way into life and truth is a path called Jesus. And we have to "get on" the path who is Jesus if we hope to ever find the life we long for and the truth we were created to love. The constant enemy of this pursuit is always "I already know him," while our trusted friend is always "I know next to nothing about him." We must denounce the former and embrace the latter.

In his excellent book *Jesus Mean and Wild,* Mark Galli describes this denouncing/embracing rhythm. Galli was pastor of a California church when a group of Laotian refugees asked if they could become members. Galli offered to lead them through a study of Mark's Gospel as a foundational exercise before they made their commitment. The Laotians had little knowledge of Scripture or of Jesus. When Galli got to the passage where Jesus calms the storm, he asked the refugees to talk about the "storms" in their lives—their problems, worries, and struggles. The people looked confused and puzzled. Galli filled the awkward silence by asking, "So what are your storms?"

Finally, one of the Laotian men asked, "Do you mean that Jesus actually calmed the wind and sea in the middle of a storm?" Galli thought the man was merely expressing his skepticism, and because he wasn't intending to spend the group's remaining time wrestling with the plausibility of Jesus' miracles, he said: "Yes, but we should not get hung up on the details of the miracle. We should remember that Jesus can calm the storms in our lives."

After another uncomfortable stretch of silence, another man spoke up: "Well, if Jesus calmed the wind and the waves, he must be a very powerful man!" The Laotians buzzed with excitement about this while Galli looked on as a virtual outsider. While these newbie Christian refugees entered into something like worship, Galli realized he'd so taken Jesus for granted that he'd missed him altogether.[26]

When we think we know everything there is to know about Jesus, then we move into the "Jesus-plus" mode. We're "been there, done that" with Jesus, so we turn our attention to the tips and techniques that will make our life work better. So, sure, we follow Jesus and are sorta/kinda focused on him, but that's not really enough for us. We need a growing list of "pluses" to hang in there with this life. And in a highly competitive cultural marketplace of "pluses," many students are "plus-ing" their way right out of relationship with Jesus. In my own journey of awakening, I wondered whether I'd done the same thing as Galli. Had I so taken Jesus for granted in my life that I'd essentially stopped relating with him as he really is? Even more, had I so "understood" Jesus that my pursuit of him was far less interesting to me than the pursuit of Christian relationships or postmodern worship or artistic expressions of the Christian life or culturally relevant approaches to Bible study?

"Who do I say Jesus is?" is much more than a question to be answered. It's the point of our life's pursuit and the navigational North Star for youth ministry. We're always heading in this direction, no matter if we have to tack to the left or right along the way. And we're always pointing our boat in this direction because there is no other Way.

Who Does Jesus Say I Am?

When Nicodemus the Pharisee visits Jesus in the cloak of darkness to ask him questions about who he is and what he intends to do, Jesus condenses all realities into one simple reality: "You must be born again." Here he's pulling back the curtain on what's really going on in our life, and in the spiritual world that encloses our physical world: We're caught up in a war that is waged on the battlefield of our identity. There is a "one true God" who loves us and is bent on restoring us into relationship with him by redeeming our broken identity. The essence of who we are must be born again. And we have a "killing, stealing, and destroying" enemy who is intent on dismantling our identity so completely that we forget we were made for God's pleasure.

This explains why so many of us—and almost all teenagers—struggle to understand and embrace our true identity as beloved children of God. In the "enemy territory" that is our life on earth, teenagers are caught in a swirl of voices, all demanding the right to *identify* them.

- The advertisers who invade every nook and cranny of their lives would like them to believe that consumption will mark their identity.

- The teachers who set their everyday agenda would like them to believe that their academic performance will frame their ongoing personal happiness.

- The coaches who intend to discipline them would like them to believe that physical pursuits define their character.

- The parents who infect them with their unique family system would like them to believe that "trying harder to get better" is the primary path to the "good life" they deserve.

- Their music would like them to believe that their sexuality and their ability to exert power over others is the real currency of life.

- Their church, if they have one, would like them to believe that mastering biblical principles will guarantee a successful trajectory in life.

- Their enemies would like them to believe that they're no more valuable than a piece of garbage.

And, of course, these are just the obvious voices. There's no space to catalog all the hundreds of identity-shaping influences kids experience every day. And God's enemy practices a strategic leverage in their lives; if he can poison their true identity by planting "destructive narratives" about who they are, they'll push the "self-destruct" button themselves. When we believe what isn't true about ourselves and live out of that momentum, we sabotage the redemptive work of God in us. Answering the question "Who does Jesus say I am?" is, literally, a life-saving pursuit. It's the voice of Jesus naming them, just as he did with Peter, that shatters the false beliefs teenagers have embraced about themselves. These include:

- "You'll never be good enough."

- "Your performance is what's important, not your effort."

- "You damage and spoil everything you touch."

- "The reason you're treated badly by others is because they see who you really are."

- "People will always let you down, so you'd better protect yourself with self-reliance."

- "The reflection you see in the mirror is so flawed that you may never find someone to love you."

Jesus made his mission and purpose clear: "I have come to set captives free" (Luke 4:18). And what is our captivity defined by? The false identity that our sin forms in us. This is evident when Jesus infuriates the Pharisees (again!) by offering forgiveness, not healing, to a paralytic man whose friends have brought him to the Master in hopes of a miraculous physical restoration. Jesus responds with this: "Which is easier: to say, 'Your sins are forgiven,' or to say, 'Get up and walk' "? (Matthew 9:5). Our core need is forgiveness that leads to a restoration of relationship that cements our true identity as God's beloved. We are as equally paralyzed by the damage to our identity as we are damaged by physical paralysis. To Jesus, they're the same thing. And his knee-jerk response to our gaping needs is, always, to bring truth and light to our identity. Jesus wants to answer our students' deepest question, which is: "Who am I, and am I treasured?"

Teenagers are constantly checking themselves in their cultural mirrors. They use a wide variety of reflective materials to get a glimpse of who they really are. Their "mirrors" include their number of Facebook friends, how fast a friend texts them back, how well they're able to attract the attention of the opposite sex, their mile-run time, their GPA, the number and prestige of their college acceptance letters, and on and on. Teenagers are surrounded by mirrors, and almost all of those mirrors give a false reflection of their true beauty. In truth, every mirror except for one is a funhouse mirror; I mean, they're all warped at least a little, and therefore present a false image. The one exception is Jesus. He alone is a pristine and accurate mirror for who we really are.

This is why *both* orbital questions must be embedded in our ministry. The first is about knowing Jesus; the second is about knowing ourselves in the light of Jesus. When students know Jesus and know themselves, they are dangerous-for-good. That's just another way of saying they're disciples of Jesus, the most powerful force for transformation and redemption on the face of the earth.

Protecting Our Kids From Jesus
By Duffy Robbins

I'd been scheduled to speak at a large regional denominational event out West, and about two weeks before the event I received a call from a woman on the "design team." She wanted to review with me some basic details of the conference schedule and travel plans. It was pretty routine. That's when she added, without any hint of irony, this additional direction: "Please, when you give your talks to the kids, we've decided as a design team to ask that you not mention the name of Jesus. We don't mind if you talk about God; in fact, we hope you will. But we hope you'll understand that talking about Jesus will offend some of our young people, and we don't want to do anything that will make them feel uncomfortable...."

I tried to imagine a doctor who refused to tell her patient of his disease because it might, after all, trouble him. Or the spelling teacher who didn't have the heart to tell his students they were consistently misspelling certain words because he didn't want to discourage them. Or the traffic cop who couldn't bring himself to ask the driver to please keep his truck off the sidewalk because he didn't want the driver to think he was unfriendly. In my mind's eye, I saw the furrowed brows of the design-team members as they wrestled with "the Jesus problem."

Today, modesty seems as out of date as Pong and penny loafers—no topic is taboo, no indignation untelevised, no truth held back. That's why it's striking that we in the church have finally found a modesty we can feel good about: We can be modest about Jesus. I'm entirely sympathetic with the motives that must have led these good folks to "design" the Designer out of their youth event. After all, they wanted to make the conference a safe place for kids to ask questions and feel accepted and comfortable. I agree with that. But just because we want all patients—no matter how sick—to feel welcomed into the hospital, we don't withhold the cure because we're afraid of offending the virus. This is when a "generous orthodoxy" becomes a "disingenuous orthodoxy."

Several years ago I heard that the archbishop of Canterbury said the Church of England was "dying of good taste." I hope it's not in poor taste to say so, but I fear the same may be happening to us in youth ministry. One of the great temptations in youth ministry is to keep our kids safe. So we concentrate on nice little programs—stuff that's affirming and won't offend anybody. We try not to talk too much about sin. We avoid God's harder edges. And for pity's sake, let's go low-key when we talk about Jesus. It reminds me of one of the great scenes in C.S. Lewis' *The Lion, the Witch, and the Wardrobe,* when the children first hear about Aslan, the mysterious, frightening Christ-figure who's rumored to be on the prowl.

> "Is—is he a man?" asked Lucy.

> "Aslan a man!" said Mr. Beaver sternly. "Certainly not.
> I tell you he is the King of the wood and the son of
> the great Emperor-Beyond-the-Sea. Don't you know

who is the King of Beasts? Aslan is a lion—the Lion, the great Lion."

"Ooh!" said Susan, "I'd thought he was a man. Is he—quite safe? I shall feel rather nervous about meeting a lion."

"That you will, dearie, and no mistake," said Mrs. Beaver, "if there's anyone who can appear before Aslan without their knees knocking, they're either braver than most or else just silly."

"Then he isn't safe?" said Lucy.

"Safe?" said Mr. Beaver. "Don't you hear what Mrs. Beaver tells you? Who said anything about safe? 'Course he isn't safe. But he's good. He's the King, I tell you."[27]

I never agreed in that phone call to refrain from talking about Jesus. I couldn't. First of all, that's not me. And second, that's not the gospel. I *did* do the event, and I *did* talk about Jesus (a little more than normal). And what we all experienced that weekend, once again, was Jesus Christ meeting the desperate yearnings of kids restless and helpless in their adolescent storms. He's *not* safe, but oh he is so good.

—*Duffy Robbins is a Professor of Youth Ministry at Eastern University.*

On Teaching Teenagers the Faith

In an address to the International Youth Forum, Harvard law professor Mary Ann Glendon said: "If religious formation does not come up to the general level of secular education, we are going to run into trouble defending our beliefs—even to ourselves. We are going to feel helpless when we come up against the secularism and relativism that are so pervasive in our culture and in the university. We are going to be tongue-tied when our faith comes under unjust attack."[28]

The churches studied in the *Exemplary Youth Ministries* project couldn't agree more, and they're doing something about it:

- "Here we talk about everyday situations, like, you can pick out things happening at school and they can help you relate Scripture to everyday life."

    —A teenager at First United Methodist Church in Valparaiso, Indiana

- "Our real responsibility is in discipleship to help [our young people] discover what their faith is like—not mine, not the pastor's, not their parents. The point of our youth group is: *How does your faith attach to your life? How do your decisions reflect your relationship with God?*"

    —Kerry Gruizenga, youth minister at First Presbyterian Church in Billings, Montana

- "We talk about things that matter.... We talk about how to talk about your faith, world religions, and our own questions about faith."

  —A teenager at Thornapple Evangelical
  Covenant Church in Grand Rapids, Michigan

- "The genius behind [the ministry] is that they're intentional about going deep, and they've replicated with others who can share the burden with them. They've purposely done that instead of being biggest, flashiest, showiest. The purpose here is going deep."

  —A parent at Newport Mesa Christian Center in
  Costa Mesa, California

Part Two
Beeline Practices

Jesus practiced what contemporary educators would call an "inquiry-based" teaching strategy. Put more simply, he asked lots of questions, forcing his followers to think and explore and pursue. An inquiry-based approach is proven to engage students at a deeper (but much more accessible) level than conventional "lecture" strategies. Educational reformer Joe Exline explains the traction of an inquiry-based approach: "Memorizing facts and information is not the most important skill... Facts change, and information is readily available—what's needed is an understanding of how to get and make sense of the mass of data... [We] need to go beyond data and information accumulation and move toward... useful and applicable knowledge, a process supported by inquiry learning. Inquiry implies a 'need or want to know' premise. Inquiry... implies emphasis on the development of inquiry skills and the nurturing of inquiring attitudes or habits of mind that will enable individuals to continue the quest for knowledge throughout life." [29]

The shift to a two-question Jesus-centered youth ministry will mean that everything you do revolves around the pursuit of these questions, and that will naturally drive an inquiry-based approach. You'll need a critical mass of ministry practices that make these two questions the focus, and you'll need to shift away from "talking at" teenagers to asking lots more questions that encourage them to pursue Jesus. In the last half of this book, we'll explore how to embrace and live out an array of practices that will create an orbital center around the pursuit of Jesus in your ministry. In my experience, and in the experience of thousands of youth workers who've gone through this training, your enjoyment of what you do and how you do it will go way up. And as these practices become the norm, the gravitational pull you've created around Jesus will grow stronger and stronger. Plus, as kids get closer and closer to Jesus, the fruit will start flying off of them.

Of course, not all of these practices will fit your ministry or your particular leadership style, but most will. Tremendous flexibility is built into them. So I invite you to climb on this bike and push on the pedals. It'll be wobbly at first, but you'll be flying down the street with the wind in your face before you know it. And to help set a little "in the trenches" context for each of these practices, I've asked my friend and longtime respected "ministry practitioner" Kurt Johnston, student ministries pastor at Saddleback Church in Southern California, to describe how his ministry is leaning into this Jesus-centered approach. Look for his short "In Practice" pieces at the end of every chapter.

CHAPTER SIX
BEELINE THE BIBLE

"Christ is not valued at all, unless he is valued above all."
 —St. Augustine

C.H. Spurgeon would make a great youth pastor in today's cultural and ministry climate, because he advocated a kind of prophetic simplicity. As never before, we're distracted by the swirl of "normal life," characterized by overwhelming "shoulds" and impossible-to-process torrents of information. Because of this, we are daily more addicted to shallow insights and reactionary narratives. We live in Twitter-bites, where complex and nuanced issues are reduced to platitudes and polemics. Life is hyper-stimulating, and it's making us thin-of-soul.

In *Death by Suburb,* a countercultural call-to-arms for a people overwrought by the pace and demands of contemporary life, author Dave Goetz advocates something he calls "the thicker life." This way of living is marked by a primary abandonment to Jesus, a desperate dependence on his centering guidance, and an outward focus on the needs of others. "Thick" is a slow-down-and-pay-attention way of life, and it's in stark contrast to the speed-up-and-fibrillate way of life that has become commonplace.

Spurgeon was scorned by the "Pharisees" of his time; they accused him of pandering to the "proletariat" by oversimplifying the Christian life. But one man's oversimplifying is another man's prophetic vision. Spurgeon was, indeed, an advocate of a life and a ministry that's stripped down to its high-performance Ferrari engine: "A sermon without Christ as its beginning, middle, and end is a mistake in conception and a crime in execution."[30] Spurgeon's beeline focus transcends flash-in-the-pan ministry trends and experiments.

Though we're always drawn by hopeful curiosity to what might be called "ministry success narratives," researchers who conducted the *Study of Exemplary Congregations in Youth Ministry*[31] discovered that a single-minded, persistent, saturating focus on Jesus Christ marked the most effective ministry cultures. The three-year study combined quantitative research with qualitative insights drawn from intensive site visits to the targeted youth ministries. They focused on churches in seven major denominations that had become known within their circles as "exemplary"— profoundly "successful in shaping the faith lives of youth."

Pastors and youth pastors connected to exemplary youth ministries were asked to complete this sentence: "The youth ministry of our congregation would die if..." A common response was: "If the ministry's emphasis shifts away from its focus on Jesus Christ." The kindred pursuit of these exemplary youth ministries is summed up by an adult volunteer at Rochester Covenant Church in Minnesota, one of the churches in the study: "The genius [of our youth ministry] is a passion for Christ. Everything else just falls into place." These ministries live in the spirit of the Apostle

Paul, who condensed his life's ambitions into one sentence in 1 Corinthians 2:2: "For I determined to know nothing among you except Jesus Christ, and Him crucified." Sounds radically oversimplified, doesn't it? But oversimplified, in this case, is the doorway into the kingdom of God. The beeline leads us past our clamoring distractions and into the heart of Jesus, where every treasure we've ever longed for is buried.

So to create a "thicker" environment for youth ministry, we'll need to start with the primary practice of beelining the Bible. Instead of approaching Bible study or Bible teaching from a life-application angle, we use interesting topics—and every Bible passage—as the first step on a path toward Jesus. No matter where we're studying in the Bible, or what topic we're studying, we always—*always*—find a beeline to Jesus.

This is no theoretical possibility; it's a practical reality. As I train youth workers to beeline the Bible in their ministries, I ask one person at each table to close their eyes, open a Bible, and pick a random passage. Then, together with others at the table, the blind Bible-stabber has just five minutes to identify the beeline to Christ from the random passage and brainstorm a plan to teach that passage in a Jesus-centered way. I mean, no matter what the passage, the idea is to put that passage in the context of Jesus' life and ministry. If the random passage is a random road in England, how do you get from there to the "London" of Jesus?

I always love it when a table gets "stuck" with something from Ezekiel or (horrors!) Leviticus. But in *every single case*, after almost a decade of experimenting with this, youth workers who are at first skeptical—as skeptical about the beeline as that young preacher who Spurgeon critiqued—discover a certain path from wherever they land in the Bible to the "metropolis of Christ." Some groups are so excited by this experiment that they choose to dive into the Bible a second time if their first round seems too easy.

When you beeline every single Bible reference back to Jesus, somehow or someway you create a buzz of anticipation and even a sense of awe and worship. It's good to remember that John's Gospel tells us Jesus is "the Word." Jesus' fingerprints are all over the Bible. There's a built-in beeline to Jesus no matter where you go in Scripture. And it's our imperative (and our grand adventure) to find it. Simply put, our challenge is to never again teach from the Bible, or plan a Bible study, or launch into a topical study of any kind, without making a beeline to Jesus. Never again.

As I've already warned, this practice will feel a little clunky at first. But it won't take long before it feels "normal"—and you won't be able to go back to your old patterns of Bible study or teaching. The difference between walking from point A to point B and, instead, peddling a bicycle to get there is as simple as deciding to learn a new skill, then practicing it until it becomes like breathing. You don't have to think about it anymore because it's become autonomic.

Here's how the transition from walking to peddling works in the extreme, when I'm simply choosing a random passage to beeline:

First, I close my eyes, and then I stab my finger into my Bible and come up with Job 5:22. It's in the middle of a speech by Eliphaz (one of Job's "friends") titled "The Innocent Do Not Suffer." The "advice" that encompasses verse 22 (where I've added emphasis) actually starts in verse 17:

> "Blessed is the man whom God corrects; so do not despise the discipline of the Almighty. For he wounds, but he also binds up; he injures, but his hands also heal. From six calamities he will rescue you; in seven no harm will befall you. In famine he will ransom you from death, and in battle from the stroke of the sword. You will be protected from the lash of the tongue, and need not fear when destruction comes. *You will laugh at destruction and famine, and need not fear the beasts of the earth.*"

So I close my eyes again and pray: *God, where is the beeline?* In a moment, I have it (I'm sure there are many more ways to go with this, but this is the one that surfaces for me in this moment): "What does Jesus *really* promise us?" I'd compare Eliphaz's view of a God who punishes the bad and rewards the good to Jesus' mission to love even his enemies. And I'd scan the Gospels to pluck out every promise Jesus made and compare them to what Eliphaz *represents* as God's promises. That's the beeline.

I've now trained thousands of youth pastors to do what I just did. And it's normally a lot easier to do than the experiment I just shared with you, because we're not choosing random

Scripture passages when we teach or study. The effect of finding the beeline every time we crack open the Bible (or tap on our Bible app) is that we sink into the truth Spurgeon discovered: that all roads lead to the metropolis of Christ. And students who are immersed in this beelined-Bible environment soon adopt it into their spiritual DNA. It changes forever the way they view Scripture study, mission trips, service projects, games, retreats, and, most importantly, their everyday lives. And it will flip a switch in them that can't be turned off, one that enables them to find Jesus—or the kingdom of God he describes—everywhere they look.

IN PRACTICE

Beelining the Bible

Our youth ministry is right now taking baby steps as we learn to beeline the Bible. After I participated, for the first time, in an exercise Rick led, I've been on a mission (a baby-step mission) to proactively work Jesus into every lesson I teach. I've done this the easy way, the harder way, and the hardest way.

Easy Way—Our junior high small group curriculum is now 100 percent dedicated to helping students learn about Jesus together. When Jesus is the topic, it's pretty easy to make a beeline to him!

Harder Way—In our weekly large-group teaching time, regardless of the topic (we do a lot of topical teaching in this setting), I've asked everybody who teaches to loop in what Jesus had to say that might apply to the topic at hand. We try not to force our topic into Jesus' teachings, but our starting point now is to assume he had insight into the topic.

Hardest Way—The Bible-beelining practice Rick describes is a discipline we've started in our ministry, though not perfected. But we're determined to help our students discover how everything in God's Word ultimately points to Jesus.

—*Kurt Johnston*

Danger of Irrelevance?

If we're always making a beeline to Jesus, what do we do about the issues—the problems and challenges—facing our teenagers? Drug and alcohol abuse? Sexual activity? The push to succeed? Divorce? Depression? Stress? Cultural influences? This is exactly the issue the young preacher, flabbergasted and annoyed, was targeting when he told Spurgeon: "We are not to be preaching Christ always, we must preach what is in the text."

Up until now, most of us have been like overworked pruners in a fast-growing orchard. We scurry around trying to cut off the bad fruit we see around us. We do teaching series on sex, on money, on music and movies, on relationships... on and on. The truth is, as kids come to know Jesus more deeply and begin to abide in him as the "root" of their lives, their fruit will change. They will be transformed "by the renewing of [their] mind" (Romans 12:2). We won't have to run around cutting off rotten fruit!

But that's not to say we won't need to focus on these topics. We'll just focus on them with the goal of helping teenagers find and experience the beeline to Jesus. Simply brainstorm (alone or with help) the topics students are most interested in learning about and those we think are important for them to hear. Then find the beeline to Jesus for each one.

CHAPTER SEVEN
CREATE DEPENDENT EXPERIENCES

"Teenagers have more information about God than they have experiences of him. Get them in places where they have to rely on God." —Timothy Keller

And now for something completely different...

A few summers ago, Colorado youth pastor Josh Jones decided it was time to lurch his ministry out of its summer-mission-trip rut. Every year they'd load up their 12-passenger van and head south for the 28-hour trek to Mexico and a weeklong work camp. And every year, as they traveled through countless towns and cities on the way to their mission focus, they saw dozens of ministry opportunities they were forced to pass by. Those "on the way" possibilities planted the seed of an idea in Josh and his teenagers. So on the heels of a semester-long teaching series that focused on a dependent relationship with the Holy Spirit, Josh gathered his students for something he called The Magical Mystery Tour. The experience would replace their annual summer mission trip and would change his group forever.

Here's a condensed description of the trip, from Josh's own account:

Because we'd been learning about dependence on the Holy Spirit, we decided we didn't need a "destination" for our trip. Simply, we decided to ask the Holy Spirit to lead us to where he wanted us to go... We had no destination in mind and no plans for where we were going to stay or eat—all we had were a lot of "what if's" and a trailer-full of supplies hitched to our van. Before we loaded up to leave, we met inside the church for breakfast and an extended time of prayer. We encouraged each other to keep our eyes open to opportunities we'd normally overlook. And we began a 24-hour fast after breakfast to help us focus on following the Spirit's lead. Then we stood in the parking lot and asked God to show us where to go. One of our teenagers tossed a pebble onto a map that she couldn't see from where she was standing. In four out of five tosses, the pebble landed in the exact same spot—Northwest Colorado. So we buckled up and headed west.

As we drove into the mountains, we saw a moving truck broken down on the side of the road. One of our teenagers asked if we could stop to see if there was anything we could do for them. We pulled over and introduced ourselves to a couple who were moving from Vermont to California, following God's call in their lives, to begin working at an orphanage as house parents. The woman started to cry as she told their story. The breakdown had made them question whether they'd made the right decision. The man was anxious and worried about the truck. We couldn't help them mechanically, but we prayed for them, gave them a few bottles of water, and encouraged them. We told them where the next town with a mechanic was (only a mile or two up the road), and we were on our way.

We pulled in to Grand Junction, Colorado, and decided to drive through town with "open eyes" to see what we could find. One of our girls noticed an empty lot covered in trash and asked if we could stop and pick up the trash. As we finished cleaning the lot, we saw there was a hospital across the street, so we decided to go see if there was anything we could do at the hospital on a Saturday evening. A woman at the front desk told us that because of privacy rules we couldn't pop in unannounced to patient rooms, but she was so impressed with what we were trying to do that she gave us the name and phone number of a local church. When we pulled up to the church, people were just filing out of the Saturday evening service. Some of our group went inside to see if they could find a lead on some way we could serve. When our kids described what we were doing, a couple of congregants asked, "Do you have a place to stay tonight?" Well, that was God's grace to us because it was starting to get dark, and the nearest campground was over an hour away. Church leaders told us they had several projects that needed workers, including washing out a bus, bagging up 100 meals for church-sponsored students, preparing food to feed over 200 homeless people on Sunday afternoon (remember, we were fasting!), and painting their enormous children's ministry room. So we got to work and praised God that he had directed us to a place that not only needed help, but was also an example to us of reaching out to others in their community.

From Saturday night through Tuesday morning, we worked at this church completing our projects. Not only did they provide us with a place to sleep and showers for three nights, they also fed us well. God truly provided for us! Tuesday morning, we all felt God was calling us to leave Grand Junction, so we prayed some more and then spun a Twister wheel that had "north, south, east, and west" on it. The arrow landed on east, so we followed Highway 50, which runs slightly southeast. After two more stops along the highway to help travelers with flat tires, it was almost time for lunch. As we pulled in to Montrose, Colorado, we noticed that all the flags were at half-staff. We found a newspaper and read that a police officer with the Montrose Police Department had been shot and killed while responding to a domestic violence call on Saturday night, and two other officers had been injured in the incident. So our group decided to go to the police station to see if there was anything we could do for the department, the families, or the community.

The police commander came out and told us there really wasn't anything they needed us to do, but he was very touched by our offer. We then asked if we could pray with him for his department and the families of the injured and dead. He started tearing up as he listened to Justin (son of a police officer) pray for him and his fellow officers. *[The group continued on into Utah, then back into Colorado for a series of similar "apparently random" ministry opportunities and acts of grace.]*

Saturday morning we drove home to Denver. After we pulled into the church parking lot, we gathered inside the church for a short time of worship, thanking God for the way he'd provided for us and moved through us to meet needs throughout the week. And we prayed that the things we had done that week would bring lasting impact—that our "never-ending mission" mind-set would spill into our everyday lives as we listened and responded to the Spirit. It truly was an amazing week. I think our teenagers got a real sense of God's provision in their lives, what it means to have their eyes open to others' needs, and how to follow the Spirit's guiding in their lives. Our group has never been the same since our Magical Mystery Tour. Nothing we've ever done has impacted their relationship with Jesus so deeply.

That weeklong experiment in Spirit-dependence is a super-charged example of an everyday practice that reorients our lives from self-reliance to Jesus-attachment. Dependent experiences like the Magical Mystery Tour shove teenagers into a viscerally reliant relationship with Jesus, and that radically deepens their attachment to him. That's why dependent experiences are at the heart of a Jesus-centered ministry. Churches that create or facilitate them for students embed an engine of growth that propels everything they do. For example, researchers discovered that the 21 "exemplary" youth ministries they identified in the United States have made an art form out of inviting their students to depend on Jesus. They put their kids in the "hot seat" of ministry leadership and participation, rather than the "cold seat" of ministry consumption.

- When Johnny Derouen was leading the youth ministry at Travis Avenue Baptist Church in Fort Worth, Texas, his passion was to hand off responsibility to his students so they could learn how to depend on the Spirit of Jesus, then act out of that leading: "My job is to teach the students and adults and parents... how to do ministry. I give it back to them, and it is their ministry.... The high school students are trained at school to do things by themselves, and I'm not going to do it for them when they get here. The whole program is geared to push you to the next level.... By the time you are a junior or senior you are leading the program, you're leading small groups, mission-trip groups, you're running the programs. You don't have to, but it is expected—it leads to maturity."

- An adult volunteer at New Colony Baptist Church in Billerica, Massachusetts, says: "We had students writing their own psalms. And one of our youth leaders put it to music and made a whole CD of kids' songs." Another volunteer leader at New Colony adds, "The kids take such ownership. They plan and help with the worship and then lead the rest of the group. They've made songs, a movie. We're doing an experience tomorrow—it's not us standing in front of them telling them what to say and what to do."

- A teenage girl at Newport Mesa Christian Center in Costa Mesa, California, once wrote, as a joke, that she'd like to play cowbell during the worship time. "I was totally kidding. But next week Lynette [the youth pastor] gave me a cowbell and I was playing during worship. I didn't even know how to play. If you want to lead clapping during worship, they will make a place for you."

The practice of creating dependent experiences for students simply means we find ways to place ourselves, and students, in God-dependent situations. That means we must risk the pristine results we're sure our own efforts will produce and opt for the messy unknown of teenagers learning how to trust Jesus and experiment their way into the unknown. Simply, we're nudged toward dependence on God when we're placed in dependent circumstances.

Scaring Students for Good

Post-college, I joined an international training school to learn how to be a cross-cultural street evangelist. One night in Sicily during an outreach event, a woman came screaming and flailing into our midst, apparently possessed by a demon. There was no time to flip through the field manual at that point. And, also, there's no field manual for cross-cultural demon-possession prayer.

My other wide-eyed missionary friends and I had to trust that the Spirit of Jesus would show us what to do as we were doing it. And we did. We prayed over her as best we could, trusting Jesus to assert his authority. And the woman promptly stopped screaming and frothing and thrashing. She became calm, as if someone had flipped a switch inside her. We stood amazed at the power of God held in "earthen vessels."

In practical terms, "as-we're-doing-it ministry" means scaring ourselves and our teenagers—in a good way. It means plunging into risks that the Spirit puts before us. In terms of student ministry, it might mean asking kids to lead something that we'd normally lead, or serve in a setting that's far outside their comfort zone, or reach out to people whose problems are beyond their ability to solve, or introduce others to the real Jesus.

And one simple way to move kids from independence to dependence is to change the way we teach them to pray. A.W. Tozer once said: "If you do all the talking when you pray, how will you ever hear God's answers?" So instead of simply "brainstorming" our prayers, we stop first and pause in silence to ask Jesus to guide us. It's a simple "How should I pray, Jesus?" Then we wait, then we pray accordingly. Such dependent prayer is almost unheard of in the church. In one of Group Magazine's recent nationwide surveys of Christian teenagers, kids described "talking" as their primary prayer activity; very few of them listed "listening." The more we model dependent prayer for our students, the closer they will get to Jesus. Listen first, then pray.

Our path to dependence follows the trail Peter blazed. We (and teenagers) listen when Jesus calls and get out of our "boat" to walk on water to him. If we do this often enough, we'll develop an easy dependence on Jesus that gives us an ever-deepening taste of him. My friend Ron Belsterling, a professor of youth ministry at Nyack College in New York, told me about an experience that profoundly sealed his perspective on the power of dependent experiences to create a Jesus-centered mentality in his ministry. As part of a doctoral project, Ron had convinced his church to experiment with an outreach trip that targeted a nearby inner-city neighborhood. This replaced the youth group's traditional overseas trip that included four days of "ministry" and six days of fun on the beach. Parents who were fine about their kids going on a cross-cultural mission/fun trip were very worried about them walking the streets of an urban neighborhood that was just 20 minutes away.

One night Ron and the kids on his inner-city outreach looked out their hotel window and saw two men viciously kicking a woman who was high on drugs, and therefore unable to defend herself or run away. Ron turned to these protected, wide-eyed, middle-class teenagers and asked, "What are we going to do about this?"

The kids said, "Well, we can't go down there!"

Ron answered, "Why not? *Down there* is where Jesus would be."

The students responded: "What can we do? The only thing we know how to do is sing!" (Most of the kids on the outreach were part of the church's respected youth choir.)

Ron fired back, "Well, let's go down there and sing then. We'll give what Jesus has given us to give."

So the whole group trooped down to the street, stood on the opposite sidewalk, and started singing. The two guys kicking the woman looked up, startled, and then immediately ran away in fear. The woman then crawled across the street and lay down in the middle of the kids as they continued singing. That night, those kids followed the beeline that Ron found for them. They learned what it's like to follow the nudge of the Spirit and offer rescue to a woman in trouble, just as Jesus did with the woman caught in adultery in John 8. And the wall separating their faith from their real life crumbled a little more.

A Hunger for a `Bigger Ask´

Today's young people have a hunger to live more dependently, responding to the Spirit of Jesus in their lives. One teenager who's part of an "exemplary youth ministry" at Travis Avenue Baptist Church in Fort Worth, Texas, told an interviewer: "Service is being Christlike, and we are taught to live a Christlike walk. It isn't how you achieve it; it is a result of it." A teenager involved in another exemplary youth ministry, at Thornapple Evangelical Covenant Church in Grand Rapids, Michigan, wrote this note to her dad about her experience on an outreach trip to Washington, D.C.:

Dear Dad,

I have a story that I really think you'll like, so I hope you read this. This morning was the first morning at a mission site. I was chosen to go to the earliest site, 6:30 a.m., to Third Street Church. It is a food kitchen in the bottom of the church. We started out by talking to the homeless who were there waiting for food, then singing, and preparing breakfast while listening to a sermon.... I was in charge of giving one drink to every person in line who wanted one, but we were limited on supplies. Whatever we poured out was whatever we had, and we had only enough to fill three trays. We had so many people in the shelter that we sadly had to close the doors and turn people away. I looked around the room and was really worried that we would not have enough juice for everyone.... I prayed right away that God would provide at least one for every person in the mission. The line formed and everyone started to come through. I kept praying and trusting that God would provide. Then everyone was able to come up and get seconds, some even took thirds! We had plenty of juice for EVERYONE to have their fill, and when we cleaned everything up and most everyone had left, I noticed I had ONE extra juice! I thought it was amazing how abundantly God provided, and I felt like I had experienced a tiny bit of the feeding of the 5,000 with only a few loaves of bread and fish.

When this teenager was challenged to depend on Jesus to come through, she not only discovered something about him, she also learned something about herself. The hunger that kids have to plunge into dependent experiences is, in part, a hunger to do something really big with their lives. Look at the example of the 24-7 Prayer movement. A youth pastor in Britain couldn't get teenagers to show up for a little 30-minute prayer meeting, yet when he challenged them to pray all day, every day for several months, kids came out of the woodwork to join in. Now there are 24-7 Prayer "boiler rooms" all over the world, with tens of thousands of teenagers praying around the clock for their friends, families, and communities.[32]

At the core of our Jesus-dependence is a commitment to humility and a determination to act obediently in the moment. While attending a Short-Term Missions Forum sponsored by the National Network of Youth Ministries, I was reminded of this truth. Forum participant Sherwood Lingenfelter, provost and professor of anthropology at Fuller Seminary, threw a bolt of truth into a heated discussion about the real value of short-term missions when he said the first question we should be asking is this: "What is God already doing, and how can we partner with him in doing it?"[33]

Lingenfelter is speaking the language of Jesus, who said this to the Pharisees who were already seething at his outlandish proclamations of intimacy with his Father: "When you have lifted up the Son of Man, then you will know that I am the one I claim to be and that I do nothing on my own but speak just what the Father has taught me. The one who sent me is with me; he has not left me alone, for I always do what pleases him" (John 8:28-29).

Jesus humbled his own agenda in favor of supporting his Father's momentum and agenda—"I always do what pleases him." To do that he was always, always consulting his Father, then acting on his guidance. And we help teenagers cement their attachment to Jesus when we move them into dependent experiences where they can "test out" their relationship with him.

Jesus Seeding Dependence

Jesus was always plunging his disciples into dependent experiences. We can learn everything we need to know about how he practiced this imperative from Matthew 10, when Jesus sent out the Twelve two by two on their first ministry trip without him.

1. Jesus conferred on the disciples the spiritual authority they needed to do the job. "He called his twelve disciples to him and gave them authority to drive out evil spirits and to heal every disease and sickness" (Matthew 10:1). How is the way we ask teenagers to step up and fill important responsibilities any different from the way their teachers, coaches, or employers ask them to do the same? Well, it's unlikely any of them would lay hands on them and formally confer spiritual authority on them. The point is to publicly recognize that they've been called out or "set apart" for these responsibilities and that they won't be doing their work under their own authority or power. The book *Judaism for Dummies* describes the Hebrew word *s'michah*—the laying on of hands—this way: "*S'michah* is a way of conferring the authority of leadership from one person to another. First seen in Moses' transferring leadership of the Hebrews to Joshua just prior to entering the Holy Land, *s'michah* now refers to ordaining rabbis (where the laying on of hands is still performed)."[34]

2. Jesus started them out with a doable challenge. "These twelve Jesus sent out with the following instructions: 'Do not go among the Gentiles or enter any town of the Samaritans. Go rather to the lost sheep of Israel'" (Matthew 10:5-6). Rather than forcing them into a cross-cultural challenge or an environment of stiff resistance, Jesus started them off in familiar surroundings with familiar people. Later on they'd go "to the ends of the earth," but for now the challenge to risk and depend on the Spirit needed to be small enough to ensure some level of success.

When I was learning how to be a street evangelist in Europe, our trainers started us off by teaching us a discussion-starting drama we could perform to attract a crowd. The first place we did it was a public piazza in Rome that was well known as a gathering place for young people interested in conversation with Americans. All of us were already scared to do something that seemed so risky, but we weren't overwhelmed by our dependent challenge because we started with baby steps. We did the drama, and it provided an easy way to strike up a conversation with strangers. The bridge from shy, scared, awkward guy to international missionary was relatively easy because my leaders understood how to give us a taste of dependent living, not fire-hose us with it.

3. Jesus gave the disciples specific boundaries for their responsibilities. "As you go, preach this message: 'The kingdom of heaven is near.' Heal the sick, raise the dead, cleanse those who have leprosy, drive out demons" (Matthew 10:7-8a). If we're releasing kids to thrive on dependent experiences, they'll need specific expectations from us. Jesus went so far as to tell his disciples exactly what he wanted them to say and gave them four ministry responsibilities that very definitely required them to depend on God's power. He also, by the way, spent a lot of time modeling these responsibilities, giving the disciples plenty of time to learn how to do them from an incredible Mentor.

4. Jesus told them to expect God to meet their needs along the way. "Freely you have received, freely give. Do not take along any gold or silver or copper in your belts; take no bag for the journey, or extra tunic, or sandals or a staff; for the worker is worth his keep" (Matthew 10:8b-10). Jesus understood that ministry is all about generosity. We give out of generous hearts, and we receive from God's generous heart. That means we ask teenagers to give out of the fullness of what they've received and trust God to give them "manna" for their basic needs. A teenage girl at Newport Mesa Christian Center, an exemplary youth ministry, told an interviewer, "We see other [leaders] and how close they are to God, and we realize we can do it too."

5. Jesus risked by investing his trust in the disciples; he didn't shadow them as they ventured into the unknown.
"After Jesus had finished instructing his twelve disciples, he went on from there to teach and preach in the towns of Galilee" (Matthew 11:1). After Jesus had delivered his instructions to the disciples, he took off on his own ministry trip. Talk about communicating trust! Effectively, he was telling them he wasn't at all worried or anxious about how they'd fare on their adventure. I love how Joani Schultz, the chief creative officer at Group Publishing and one of my longtime mentors, frames the "price" we pay for inviting teenagers into a deeper dependency on Jesus: "Youth ministry is not about us; it's about God's passion for growing disciples. We must be willing to relinquish much of the leadership spotlight to allow kids to 'dance' (and sometimes suffer) in its glow. Young people are the visible doers. We're the humble servants. We're involved in youth ministry not for our own glory, but to satisfy a Christlike craving to see young people grow into God's dream for them."[35]

6. Jesus helped his disciples learn from their ministry adventures after the fact. When his disciples returned to download what happened on their ministry adventures, they told Jesus they were astonished by how God's Spirit had moved through them: "Lord, even the demons submit to us in your name." And Jesus engaged their experience by offering a greater context for it: "I saw Satan fall like lightning from heaven. I have given you authority to trample on snakes and scorpions and to overcome all the power of the enemy; nothing will harm you. However, do not rejoice that the spirits submit to you, but rejoice that your names are written in heaven" (Luke 10:18-20). He's basically reminding the disciples that the power they experienced when they depended on the Spirit of God came directly from him (so don't get too impressed with yourselves).

The practice of creating dependent experiences for your teenagers creates a saturating counterculture that raises expectations for everyone in the ministry. If you have teenagers who believe anything can happen because of their deepening dependence on Jesus, then it's quite likely that *anything will happen*!

IN PRACTICE

Creating Dependent Experiences

Although we're still novices at beelining the Bible in our ministry, creating dependent experiences may be what we do best. In fact, it's fair to say that helping students plunge into faith-stretching, Jesus-relying moments is at the core of our ministry DNA. It's who we are! But that's not because of my leadership. Saddleback's senior pastor, Rick Warren, is our primary influence. I've never met a person so comfortable in uncomfortable situations. Pastor Rick is completely at ease relying on God to show up in any given scenario, and that mentality has infected our church and youth group.

- We've taken seventh-graders on mission trips to Kenya, the Philippines, Rwanda, Costa Rica, and inner-city Los Angeles.

- We regularly ask (and expect) students to share the story of their faith journey in front of the rest of the group.

- We constantly tell our group, "We aren't going to do big outreach events for your friends; YOU need to tell them about Jesus and bring them to church."

- We consistently remind our students that following Jesus means refusing to play it safe.

- Over my long youth ministry career, I've never seen anything spur students' spiritual growth the way creating dependent experiences does. After all, relying on Jesus *is* sorta what being a Christian is all about, right?

—*Kurt Johnston*

CHAPTER EIGHT
TELL THE TRUTH ABOUT JESUS

"The longer you look at Jesus, the more you will want to serve Him. That is, of course, if it's the real Jesus you're looking at."
—N.T. Wright

I've already made a case for how and why teenagers have been encouraged to follow and worship a Jesus who doesn't really exist. No matter how much we wrangle with the implications of this reality, what's true is that kids typically describe Jesus in ways that have little relationship to what he *really* said and did. They think he's a nice, good man—kind of a Barney for grown-ups. He isn't the Jesus of the Bible, or even the Jesus of C.S. Lewis' *Chronicles of Narnia*, where he's retranslated into King Aslan, a ferocious-for-good lion who looms over all seven fantasy stories. Typical of Lewis' take on the character and personality of Jesus is this interchange from the end of *A Horse and His Boy,* when a fugitive boy named Shasta discovers that the fearsome challenges and heartbreaks of his journey through a dangerous land aren't as "unfortunate" as they appeared to be:

> "I do not call you unfortunate," said the Large Voice.

> "Don't you think it was bad luck to meet so many lions?" said Shasta.

"There was only one lion," said the Voice.

"What on earth do you mean? I've just told you there were at least two the first night, and..."

"There was only one: but he was swift of foot."

"How do you know?"

"I was the lion." And as Shasta gaped with open mouth and said nothing, the Voice continued. "I was the lion who forced you to join with Aravis. I was the cat who comforted you among the houses of the dead. I was the lion who drove the jackals from you while you slept. I was the lion who gave the Horses the new strength of fear for the last mile so that you should reach King Lune in time. And I was the lion you do not remember who pushed the boat in which you lay, a child near death, so that it came to shore where a man sat, wakeful at midnight, to receive you."

"Then it was you who wounded Aravis?"

"It was I."

"But what for?"

"Child," said the Voice, "I am telling you your story, not hers. I tell no one any story but his own."

"Who are you?" asked Shasta.

"Myself," said the Voice, very deep and low so that the earth shook: and again "Myself," loud and clear and gay: and then the third time "Myself," whispered so softly you could hardly hear it, and yet it seemed to come from all round you as if the leaves rustled with it.[36]

Yes, Jesus was a "nice guy" when he healed people or fed them miraculously or saved them from certain death or demon possession. He was certainly kind to children and went out of his way to be gentle with the brokenhearted. But he was also so fierce with hypocritical religious leaders and used such profane language to describe them that they conspired to execute him. He wasn't a "nice guy" when he labeled the Canaanite woman who sought healing for her daughter a "dog," or when he answered the Rich Young Ruler's innocent request for more "tips and techniques for better living" by telling him to sell all he owned and follow him, or (of course) when he used a whip to clear the Temple of the duplicitous money changers, or when he responded to Peter's pledge to protect him from harm by calling him "Satan." The Jesus of the Bible is more dangerous than nice; actually, he's more *everything* than the way he's typically described.

In another revelatory scene from one of Lewis' Narnia books— *The Voyage of the Dawn Treader*—a bratty, self-centered boy named Eustace is magically turned into a terrible, ugly dragon after he discovers an abandoned pile of dragon treasure and falls into a greedy sleep. At first the noxious boy enjoys the fear he can now produce in people as he swoops at them, breathing fire. But soon he's lonely, afraid, and miserable as a dragon. And his arm really hurts because he slipped a dragon-treasure bracelet onto his wrist before he fell asleep, and now it's constricting his much larger dragon limb. Amid his misery, Aslan comes to him in the night. Eustace is afraid of the lion, but not afraid of it eating him. It's a different kind of fear—the kind you feel when you sense a Presence much bigger and greater than yourself.

The lion leads Eustace to a well in the mountains and tells him he must "undress" before he slips into the well's soothing waters. Eustace doesn't understand what it means to "undress" at first because he's, well, already a naked dragon. But soon he figures out he should try to tear away at his dragon skin to see if he can find the boy still living underneath it. He does this three times, to no effect. Then the lion says: "You will have to let me undress you." Because Eustace is desperate, he lies on his dragon back and exposes his soft underbelly to the lion's claws: "The first tear he made was so deep that I thought it had gone right into my heart," he says. And after the lion tears away the deepest remnants of Eustace's dragon skin, he invites him into the water. When he emerges he's a boy again (actually, a boy redeemed), soon to be dressed in "new clothes" by the lion, who is Jesus Christ in full.[37]

If we polled theologians on their favorite theological works, the Narnia books would appear on many lists.[38] What Lewis did by embedding the biblical Jesus inside the character of Aslan is help us deconstruct the false Jesus of popular conception and replace that image with something closer to the truth. We have unwittingly contributed to kids' wrong impressions of Jesus by filtering the Bible's descriptions of what he said and did through our own skewed assumptions. If we, instead, simply allowed the biblical account of his personality and behavior to be our unfiltered instructor, we would find (and teach about) a Jesus who shatters our sensibilities.

G.K. Chesterton once said: "If you meet the Jesus of the gospels, you must redefine what love is, or you won't be able to stand him." This is so deeply true. Jesus was a difficult person; a lot of people were uncomfortable in his presence and scandalized by things he said and did. It's hard to "stand" Jesus if you're really paying attention to what he did and said. He is the most redemptively disruptive person who ever walked the earth. He is so much better than our typical descriptions of him, and so much more than a dispenser of life lessons or a teller of pithy fables.

The Termites Eating Away at Jesus

I've asked youth pastors all over America why it's such a challenge to connect teenagers' everyday life experiences to the experience of following Jesus. They most often say it's because contemporary culture is influencing them away from an everyday relationship with Jesus, or that students are so busy with other activities that youth group is way down the list of priorities, or that parents have dropped the ball in teaching the faith at home. These are all surface explanations that have an element of truth to them but don't get at the core problem. Most kids don't know the Jesus of the Bible very well and, therefore, don't feel compelled to go "all-in" with the Jesus they've been presented. I wouldn't go all-in with *that* Jesus, either. Plenty of nice people are doing nice things in the world, but I wouldn't give my life to follow them.

If we're not showing teenagers the real Jesus to look at, or giving them only a tiny peep at that real Jesus, they'll get a distorted, shallow, undermining sense of who he really is. That's exactly why Vintage Church in North Carolina decided to satirize the "fake Jesus" most young people have come to know—to chip away at their wrong notions of Jesus so they could be reintroduced to him. They repurposed a campy old film about Jesus by extracting four scenes from it, then recording their own dialogue to replace the original audio. The result is hilarious (you can check out the videos on YouTube by searching for "Vintage Church Jesus Videos"). They gave Jesus a falsetto Mr. Rogers voice, making him the "nice," pansy Jesus so many kids imagine anyway. Then they cleverly morphed Jesus into a distant rule-keeper who's out of touch with real life and not at all interested in an intimate relationship.

These video parodies are brilliant because they use humor to expose the false, ridiculous Jesus that teenagers often think is the true Jesus. Vintage Church understood that students would never trust this popular-but-fake Jesus with what really matters to them. The WWJD (What Would Jesus Do?) movement that I discussed earlier had a fatal flaw that remained hidden during its early momentum. If you're going to guess what Jesus would do in a particular situation (a dicey proposition anyway, when you consider how unpredictable Jesus is), everything depends on how well you know what he's already said and done. And most teenagers don't know him very well. We need a better acronym to lean into. DWKJWETKWHD stands for *Do we know Jesus well enough to know what he'd do?*

The journey toward telling the truth about Jesus starts with an honest answer to the DWKJWETKWHD question: "No, we don't know Jesus well enough to guess what he'd do in any particular situation." But this "no" offers us great hope because it will compel us to move toward deconstruction and reconstruction. This pattern is central to what Vintage Church was trying to do with those campy Jesus videos, and it's central to our commitment to tell the truth about Jesus:

1. First we deconstruct (literally tear apart) the false Jesus that's been embedded in students' hearts and minds. We do this by unearthing and confronting fallacies about him as a regular ministry practice. It's as simple as slowing down to ask our standard what/when/where/why/how questions: "What did Jesus really say/do here?" "When did he say/do it?" "Where did this all happen?" "Why did he say/do this?" "How did he say/do this?" As we question, we're digging for the truth about Jesus. We don't accept knee-jerk responses or "Christianese." We're determined to get to the bottom of Jesus, so to speak.

Our goal is to move students from patterns of lazy thinking— "We hold these truths to be self-evident"—to active engagement.

Critical thinking says, "We uphold no truths as self-evident except those that have been critically pursued and found to be in union with God's Word, both written and living." Critical and biblical thinking asks questions such as:

- Is it true from every biblical angle?

- Is it true experientially within the whole body of Christ?

- Is it true in biblical context?

- Is it true within the boundaries of things Jesus actually said and did?

- Is it true based on what I already know is true about Jesus and the kingdom of God?

- Is it true on the face of it?

- Is the foundation or source of the information true, or has it been distorted somehow?

- Is it the full truth, or does it represent only disconnected snippets of truth?

- Is it a culturally bent truth that serves a self-centered agenda?

2. Then we reconstruct and reintroduce the biblical Jesus to students, tying everything we do back into the pursuit of

him—using Spurgeon's beeline as our determined strategy.
It's an easy bridge from questioning fallacies about Jesus to embracing Chesterton's challenge to "meet the Jesus of the gospels." This will require that we redefine what love is because Jesus never did anything outside of love, even the "wounding" and "tearing" that Lewis describes in his Narnia books. We'll have to look Jesus full in the face and not shy away from the things he did that make us uncomfortable, confused, or even angry.

Adoration, Not Discipline

When we deconstruct the false Jesus who teenagers both inside and outside the church have embraced and reintroduce them to the biblical Jesus, something powerful is set in motion. We find ourselves *urging* less and *worshipping* more. I mean, a lot of what we do when we teach teenagers (and adults, really) about faith in Christ is to *urge* them to be more or do more. We're essentially pleading with them to spend more effort doing good things, to be more disciplined in their faith. But when we reintroduce Jesus in all his glory—when we slow down and pay much better attention to everything he said and did—the result is adoration. And adoration brings its own momentum with it. When we adore someone, we pay closer and closer attention to him or her.

Remember my friend Ned's "progression"? "Get to know Jesus well, because the more you know him, the more you'll love him, and the more you love him, the more you'll want to follow him, and the more you follow him, the more you'll become like him, and the more you become like him, the more you become yourself." The more teenagers worship Jesus "in spirit and truth," the more they will want to follow him, and the more their lives will naturally produce the sort of fruit we're currently urging them to manufacture through discipline.

The celebrated Christian writer Henri Nouwen served for years as pastor of Daybreak, a Christian community near Toronto for developmentally disabled people that was planted by the L'Arche movement. He wrote something about the co-founder of the L'Arche community in the United States, Father George Strohmeyer, that's a profound expression of how a "telling the truth about Jesus" environment impacts us:

> This morning I had a chance to speak with him [Father Strohmeyer] about his experience of being a priest for L'Arche.
>
> He told me about his "conversion," the main causes behind his more radical turn to Jesus. As he told his story, it became clear that Jesus was at the center of his life. George has always come to know Jesus with a depth, a richness that few priests have experienced. When he pronounces the name of Jesus you know that he speaks from a deep, intimate encounter. Since his "conversion," his life has become simpler, more hidden, more rooted, more trusting, more open, more evangelical, and more peaceful. For George, being a priest at L'Arche means leading people always closer to Jesus.

I know for sure that there is a long and hard journey ahead of me. It is the journey of leaving everything behind for Jesus' sake. I now know that there is a way of living, praying, being with people, caring, eating, drinking, sleeping, reading, and writing in which Jesus is truly the center. I know this way exists and that I have not fully found it yet.

How do I find it? George gave me the answer: "Be faithful in your adoration." He *did not say* "prayer," or "meditation," or "contemplation." He kept using the word "adoration," worship. This word makes it clear that all my attention must be on Jesus, not on myself. To adore is to be drawn away from my own preoccupations into the presence of Jesus. It means letting go of what I want, desire, or have planned, and fully trusting Jesus and his love.[39]

Teenagers caught up in the pursuit of the biblical Jesus will be inexorably drawn into an "adoration" relationship with him. In that place, they will live and breathe and move in the spirit of the first disciples—the same ones who started to believe that if they told a mountain to pick itself up and move, it would.

IN PRACTICE

Telling the Truth About Jesus

I have a mantra that our youth leadership team has heard often and everywhere: "Less God; more Jesus!" It's true that most teenagers don't know the truth about Jesus, because we simply aren't talking about him very often! Generic God-talk has replaced specific Jesus-talk. I don't know the exact percentage, but the vast majority of American teenagers believe in and like God. But Jesus? Not so much. So I've taken two simple (but in my mind, profound) steps to help rectify this:

First, in our youth group we talk about Jesus more than we talk about God. We replace "God" with "Jesus" in our lessons and language whenever it makes sense and is theologically appropriate. Perhaps a more accurate description would be that we don't talk about God less, we just talk about Jesus more than we did in the past.

Second, when we invite students to follow Jesus, we work harder than ever before to explain in detail what it means to be a Christ-follower: to admit our sin, our need for a Savior, and the truth that Jesus' death, burial, and resurrection gives us access to salvation. We've decided that we'd rather have students reject an accurate and whole presentation of the gospel than accept a shoddy one.

—*Kurt Johnston*

CHAPTER NINE

FOCUS ON THE RED STUFF

"It must be noted that Jesus alone reveals who God is... We cannot deduce anything about Jesus from what we think we know about God; however, we must deduce everything about God from what we know about Jesus." —Brennan Manning

I was standing in the checkout lane at our neighborhood grocery store, waiting to pay while the checker scanned a few things. After her initial (grunted) "hello," she paid no attention to me. Instead, she talked with a co-worker about how sick of her job she was, and how she wished she could move from a "regular" lane to the self-check lanes so she wouldn't have to interact with people.

People like me...

I was about 18 inches away from this exchange, but I felt invisible. And this wasn't a new feeling; I've noticed that at many retail outlets, the employees often seem to forget about the customer who's a few inches away. They live in a bubble that "sees" only other employees, because (it's inferred) those are the people they're most interested in building connection with.

They're home-blind. *And we who are in ministry are also often home-blind.*

Home-blind people have lost their sense of the "otherness" of Jesus—we become so acclimated to the cultural framework we've built around him, and the conventional ways we understand him, that he becomes functionally invisible. The effect is that we unconsciously push people away from him. We've spent so many years "dialing in" what we believe about Jesus that we fight against evidence that contradicts our assumptions. So we attack descriptions of him that differ from our home-blind ruts, or we functionally ignore those descriptions instead of inviting conversation around them.

Many of us have been following Jesus so long that we think we already know everything there is to know about him, so we stop exploring him in favor of topics that are of more interest to us. This, even though every survey project Group Magazine has done in the last five years that targets what teenagers want from church lists "more about Jesus" as the top vote-getter.

It's time to stir up the "sleeping giant" inside our own soul and shake ourselves awake to our own blindness. Jesus came to give sight to the blind, and all of us qualify for that gift. One profound way we can regain our sight is by focusing on the red stuff.

The Oprah Question

When I was a kid, every Bible printed the words of Jesus in red. It's a little less common today but still a popular practice. Red means "pay attention." That's why stop signs are always painted red. Designer Dustin W. Stout observes: "Red is the most eye-catching and exciting color in the entire spectrum. It's... exciting and demands attention. But did you know that the color red actually increases your heart rate? It is perfect for accent colors, calls to action, or anywhere you want to draw people's attention." [40]

So Bible publishers that print Jesus' words in red are universally on-target. Of course, all of the Bible is important to study, but the words of Jesus invite special attention because the Bible's whole narrative points to him. In a Jesus-centered youth ministry, the "red stuff" of the Bible is a staple in every context. Simply, it means we give greater focus to the things Jesus actually said.

My favorite way to focus on the red stuff is to "ask the Oprah Question." Near the back of every O Magazine, Oprah asks her celebrity guests this brilliant question: "What's one thing you know for sure?" (She asked many guests that same question on her popular talk show, too.) I've co-opted this question and extended it to this: "Based on this Scripture passage, what's one thing you know for sure about Jesus?" I'll demonstrate how this works in a moment, but first it's important to emphasize how this simple question can operate like a redemptive (red) stop sign in so many ministry arenas, not just for portions of Scripture that include Jesus' words. You can also ask the modified Oprah Question ("What do you know for sure about Jesus?") whenever you're

- debriefing a Spirit-dependent experience;

- counseling a teenager who's in crisis;

- responding to false or twisted teachings about Jesus;

- exploring ways to help students tell others about Jesus;

- tackling questions about what Jesus said and did;

- praying for others or for yourself; and

- responding to popular criticisms of Christianity.

The more you ask the question, the more it will become a natural and repetitive habit in every circumstance. You won't need to "remember to ask" because not asking will seem strange. The elegant simplicity of "What do you know for sure about Jesus?" masks its clear leverage. We think we know many things about Jesus, but what do we know for sure? It's the for sure that makes this a transformative question.

Matthew 15 and the `For Sure` Jesus

As a random exercise in asking the Oprah Question, let's try an experiment. We'll read through Matthew 15 quickly, looking for what we know for sure about Jesus as we scan through what he said and did. I'll stop writing to plunge into this right now, and I encourage you to do the same. This shouldn't take long. You're moving quickly through the red stuff and scribbling notes. Even though you're scanning, not digging, you'll need to consider this question well: "What do I know for sure about Jesus here and here and here?" Let's go...

(Elevator music.)

OK, let's compare our lists.

- Jesus likes to answer questions with questions, especially in confrontational situations.

- Jesus isn't afraid to "speak truth to power."

- Jesus is intent on smoking out hypocrisy whenever he smells the stink of it.

- Jesus uses Scripture as an anchor in contentious conversations.

- Jesus knows Scripture well enough to cite it in relevant circumstances.

- Jesus is more interested in the spirit of the Law, not the letter of the Law.

- Jesus is less interested in the words we use to represent who we are than the actions that reveal who we really are.

- Jesus decried the outward focus his people give to maintaining a righteous exterior, and he challenged them to consider what comes out of them more than what goes into them.

- Jesus is determined to expose and dismantle untruth wherever he finds it.

- Jesus knows that all truth emanates from God alone.

- Jesus is brutally choosy about the people we follow or allow to influence us.

- Jesus uses metaphor all the time to help us understand kingdom-of-God truth.

- Jesus isn't shy about confronting lazy thinking.

- Jesus has a good working knowledge of our biology and how it mirrors spiritual patterns in our life.

- Jesus often withdrew from the crowds so he could "re-center" himself.

- Jesus isn't driven by sympathy; he's intent on loving us, not sympathizing with us.

- Jesus is wildly unpredictable.

- Jesus isn't afraid to offend people.

- Jesus can be surprised and astonished by our acts of faith and persistence.

- Jesus heals people—lots and lots of people.

- Jesus is never daunted by the needs we bring to him. Nothing seems impossible to him.

- Jesus is intent on revealing the great love God has for his children.

- Jesus is aware of our physical needs, and feels compassion for them.

- Jesus doesn't let physical limitations keep him from meeting needs.

- Jesus is extravagantly generous.

Now, after this short exercise, get in touch with your own "worship level." I'm more deeply affected by the breadth and depth of who Jesus is, and I can't help myself from wanting to revel in him. Whenever we focus on the red stuff, this is the fruit that results. We're drawn like magnets to Jesus, and we give our soul something solid to feed on. And because we're simply letting the scriptural accounts speak to us, we're edging our way closer to "all-in" with him, all the time.

This simple practice—asking the Oprah Question about the red stuff—will transform the way your students relate to Jesus.

Jesus Did/Jesus Didn't

Closely related to the practice of focusing on the red stuff is another simple habit that yields similar results. I call it Jesus Did/Jesus Didn't. I'll give you a taste of how this works. Get a piece of paper and something to write with, then choose a chapter from one of the four Gospels. On your paper, draw a line down the middle to create two columns; label the first column "Jesus Did" and the other "Jesus Didn't." Then read through that chapter looking for things Jesus embraced, advised, or did, and list them under the "Jesus Did" column. Then, to spark your thinking even more, go back through that list and brainstorm the opposite of each thing you've listed. For example, if you write, "He healed people of sickness" on the "Jesus Did" side, you can write, "He didn't ignore or leave sick those who came to him seeking healing."

Let's give this practice a spin with John 6. I'll stop to do this, and then we can compare our lists again.

(Elevator music.)

Jesus Did

- Jesus is proactive about choosing when to be with crowds and when to retreat with his friends.

- Jesus tests our faith to see how we react to challenges.

- Jesus gets personally involved in meeting our needs, both spiritual and physical.

- Jesus made sure food wasn't wasted.

Jesus Didn't

- Jesus doesn't let others determine what he needs.

- Jesus doesn't always make it easy to follow him.

- Jesus doesn't "outsource" meeting needs to others.

- Jesus doesn't treat resources as things to simply throw away.

- Jesus will not be used by people who have ulterior motives.

- Jesus regularly spends time alone.

- Jesus is comfortable acting supernaturally; he exercises his authority over every "natural law."

- Jesus will both scare us and comfort us.

- Jesus understands people's hidden motivations and drags them all into the light.

- Jesus insists that we believe in him and won't offer "ironclad evidence" to convince us.

- Jesus offers us what we really need; he doesn't settle for merely what we think we need.

- Jesus doesn't "suffer fools."

- Jesus doesn't need to be around others all the time.

- Jesus doesn't make a big distinction between "natural" and "supernatural."

- Jesus doesn't always calm all our fears; he actually instigates some of them.

- Jesus doesn't ignore the games we try to play with him; he exposes them.

- Jesus doesn't answer all our questions or remove all our doubts.

- Jesus doesn't let himself be swayed by arguments that don't mesh with his will.

- Jesus doesn't always explain himself or his teaching; he forces us to wrestle with it first.

- Jesus wants a shockingly intimate relationship with us.

- Jesus defers to his Father's will, not his own.

- Jesus will say and do things that throw us into dissonance.

- Jesus is comfortable leaving people to wrestle with their doubts.

- Jesus is open, honest, and vulnerable.

- Jesus is relaxed around evil; he isn't afraid to engage it.

- Jesus doesn't mind making us uncomfortable.

- Jesus doesn't want to be our "buddy"; he wants to be our Lover.

- Jesus doesn't act arrogantly.

- Jesus isn't intent on making things easy for us.

- Jesus doesn't adjust what he says and does to make himself more palatable.

- Jesus is not an insecure person.

- Jesus isn't impressed with the threat of evil.

Just as the Oprah Question can infiltrate our engagement with students until it becomes like breathing for us, the Jesus Did/Jesus Didn't mentality can grow into a reflexive practice. Whether you use it on a broader scale (as a specific filter for a Bible study) or in a micro way (pausing to ask, "What did Jesus really do here?" and "What didn't Jesus do here?" whenever you're focusing your attention on him), it has real traction when it becomes a way of life, not a mere strategy.

This is both a deconstructing practice and a reconstructing momentum. For example, here's what happened when I searched for "Jesus healed" on BibleGateway.com. Notice what Jesus says and does, and doesn't say or do, around each healing or demon ejection (of course, this is just a sampling of the search results):

- Matthew 9:22—"Jesus turned and saw her. 'Take heart, daughter,' he said, 'your faith has healed you.' And the woman was healed from that moment."

- Matthew 12:22—"Then they brought him a demon-possessed man who was blind and mute, and Jesus healed him, so that he could both talk and see."

- Matthew 15:28—"Then Jesus answered, 'Woman, you have great faith! Your request is granted.' And her daughter was healed from that very hour."

- Mark 1:34—"And Jesus healed many who had various diseases. He also drove out many demons, but he would not let the demons speak because they knew who he was."

- Luke 9:42—"Even while the boy was coming, the demon threw him to the ground in a convulsion. But Jesus rebuked the evil spirit, healed the boy and gave him back to his father."

- John 5:13—"The man who was healed had no idea who it was, for Jesus had slipped away into the crowd that was there."

Do you notice how Jesus healed people—cared for their most desperate, temporal needs—without the kind of deal-closing behavior we look for to "legitimize" service-oriented outreach? I mean, he didn't require that people follow him or even believe in him before he healed them. That means when we love people by helping them with no strings attached, we're moving in the spirit of Jesus.

You can make the same connection to the way we engage the culture that students are immersed in. Jesus never modeled or advocated maintaining a distance from his culture. In fact, he so closely attached himself to "worldly" people and environments that some claimed he was "of the world" himself. If we think we're producing mature Christian young people by repeatedly damning popular music, contemporary books, and current movies and video games, we're confused. Hiding kids from the culture they live in, or blasting its most obviously pagan aspects, teaches them to fear it and distrust us. Either they learn to adopt a "survival" mentality that honors rigid, powerless, self-centered living over impacting the world with the truth Jesus died defending, or they develop two alter egos so they can function in both the mainstream world and the church world. Relative to cultural influences, Jesus either celebrated them or subverted them, but he didn't cloister himself from them.

A Jesus Did/Jesus Didn't mentality yields so much more fruit than the suspect practice of WWJD. Why guess about what Jesus might do when we don't yet have a firm grasp on what he's already done? When we help teenagers focus on the red stuff, we anchor their faith in reality, not conjecture.

The Real Culture War
By Walt Mueller

If you could somehow look ahead 10, 20, or 30 years and see the shape your students' faith will take as they live their adult lives, what do you hope you'd see? I'm guessing you'd want to see a mature and growing faith. But what does that really look like? And what should you be doing now to prepare them for a lifetime of mature and growing faith? A good place to start is by choosing a side in the "culture war" and equipping your students to pursue Christian maturity by doing the same for the rest of their lives.

The culture war I'm talking about isn't the one that's gotten the most press over the last few decades—that is, the culture war that's seen Christians rally the troops to fight societal problems and ideologies. Rather, it's the culture war that's been raging since Jesus ascended into heaven, the one being fought inside the walls of his church among those who call themselves his followers.

In his classic book *Christ and Culture*, H. Richard Niebuhr describes this "enduring problem" as the "many-sided debate about the relations of Christianity and civilization." To use battle language, the side you take in this war "within" shapes your approach to and level of effectiveness in your interactions with the world "without." One of the essential and most important lessons we can teach our kids is to come to an understanding of how to interact as Christ's followers with the world around them.

Throughout the course of church history and in our youth ministries today, we can see evidence of three distinct approaches to teaching and living out our relationship to culture. Which one should we model and teach to our teenagers?

When we take the approach of accommodation, we ignorantly or deliberately believe, and live out, cultural values and behaviors that are contrary to a biblical worldview. Those who accommodate the culture profess allegiance to Christ but live no differently from the world.

A more deliberate approach that's common to many youth ministries today is alienation. In this approach, our homes and youth ministries become places where we seek to protect and defend ourselves and our children from the evil and offensive influence of culture by constructing "bunkers" in which to retreat and hide.

I think these two approaches to our relationship with culture are seriously flawed. A third approach, engagement, is the one modeled and commanded by the Christ who calls us to "come and follow me"... yes, right into the culture. This approach sees the culture as a mission field ripe for redemption. The place for Christ's followers—young and old alike—is to infiltrate the world, live in the culture, and thereby exert an influence that God uses to transform individuals and institutions. Engagement allows us to communicate God's agenda in the world as those of us who've been rescued by God live redemptively in the world he made and sent his Son to redeem.

—*Walt Mueller is Founder and President of the Center for Parent/Youth Understanding.*

IN PRACTICE

Focus on the Red Stuff

OK, let's get down-and-pragmatic here. In our ministry, we practice the "practice" of focusing on the red stuff by simply focusing on the red stuff! Over the course of a typical year, our junior high and high school students explore the red stuff in many ways:

- "Flipped" is a teaching series about the way Jesus consistently flipped the world's way of thinking upside down.

- "Once Upon a Time" is a teaching series dedicated to the parables.

- "The Red Stuff" (hey, catchy title) is a teaching series that focuses on Jesus' "famous sayings."

- To any student who wants one, we provide a copy of a book by Willow Creek middle-school pastor Scott Rubin called *The Red Stuff.* This 30-day devotional helps students learn about, and learn from, the words of Jesus.

- Along with the Jesus-centered LIVE Bible (Group/ SYM), we offer students an old-school red-letter version of the Bible.

Every time a student sees the red letters in his or her Bible

and asks, "Why is some of this stuff printed in red ink?"
we're reminded that our mission is far from over.

—Kurt Johnston

CHAPTER TEN

QUESTION STRATEGIES

"The best thing you can do for your fellow, next to rousing his conscience is—not to give him things to think about, but to wake things up that are in him, or say, to make him think things for himself." —George MacDonald

Jesus practiced "inquiry-based learning" two millennia before educators in the '60s created the term. He used great questions to teach his followers how to think critically and biblically. My friend Bob Krulish, associate pastor at my church in Denver, once scoured all four Gospels to extract every single question Jesus asked. He ended up with an astonishing 287 questions! And what explosive questions Jesus asked, so potent with "wake up" leverage:

- "If a man receives circumcision on the Sabbath so that the Law of Moses may not be broken, are you angry with Me because I made an entire man well on the Sabbath?" (John 7:23, NASB).

- "I showed you many good works from the Father; for which of them are you stoning Me?" (John 10: 32, NASB).

- "Simon son of John, do you truly love me more than these?" (John 21:15).

- "Which is easier: to say to the paralytic, 'Your sins are forgiven,' or to say, 'Get up, take your mat and walk?'" (Mark 2:9).

- "Which is lawful on the Sabbath: to do good or to do evil, to save life or to kill?" (Mark 3:4).

- "How can Satan drive out Satan?" (Mark 3:23).

- "Don't you see that nothing that enters a man from the outside can make him 'unclean'?" (Mark 7:18).

- "Why then is it written that the Son of Man must suffer much and be rejected?" (Mark 9:12).

- "Salt is good, but if it loses its saltiness, how can you make it salty again?" (Mark 9:50).

- "Why do you call me good?" (Mark 10:18).

- "What then will the owner of the vineyard do?" (Mark 12:9).

I could go on and on with this list. Jesus literally peppered his followers and religious leaders with critical-thinking questions, setting explosives under the central supports propping up their false beliefs about God and his kingdom. And we can do likewise. In fact, asking good questions sounds like a no-brainer; hasn't everyone already mastered this basic skill?

Well, great critical-thinking questions about Jesus and his kingdom are rarer than we'd like to admit in youth ministry today. I was reminded of this reality all over again when a youth ministry near my Group Magazine offices agreed to let us video their small-group time for a ministry-makeover project. They agreed to let us study their youth ministry, diagnose any problems we found, and offer a "prescription" for change. We decided to confine our focus to a doable challenge by concentrating on the ministry's small groups. We worked with Jonny, the volunteer leader of the mixed-gender group for high school seniors.

When my team gathered to pore over the hours of video we took of Jonny's small group in action, one of the first things we noticed was how bad questions allowed false versions of Jesus to thrive, and how really great critical-thinking questions forced students to wrestle with the real Jesus instead. I noticed that after Jonny asked a discussion question, awkward silence often followed, or one of his kids would ask him to clarify the question. For example, in a pre-makeover small-group gathering, the topic was "The Role of the Church in Your Life." Jonny asked the group, "We just touched on something that I want you to talk about; what is church supposed to be?" Because the question was too broad and general, the kids had no idea how to answer.

We suggested to Jonny that Jesus gave the best examples of critical-thinking discussion questions, and that his questions were always surprising, specific, and personal. The more surprising, specific, and personal the question, the more likely Jonny could generate deeper Jesus-centered discussions. We challenged Jonny to make his questions more startling and more personal, and to target only one point with them.

So for the group's makeover night, Jonny asked his teenagers: "Which word comes closest to describing the way you see Jesus: nice, fierce, or mysterious? Explain." The resulting discussion was lively, intense, and long. Kids were enjoying, really enjoying, thinking about Jesus using the filter of a good critical-thinking question. Although Jonny's biggest problem had always been starting a discussion, that night he had trouble stopping it. I could see kids' false impressions of Jesus crumbling, right before my eyes.

The Art of the Ask

Most of us don't ask very good questions because we assume we already know how to ask the kinds of questions students can't stop talking about. That's the problem Jonny, our makeover youth leader, had—but he didn't know it. The solution is simply to practice creating and asking good questions until it becomes almost second nature. Let's play with this right now. I'll extract a question from a recent Bible study published in Group Magazine: "Why does God instruct believers to regularly remember Jesus' sacrifice on the cross?"

Because I've already considered and "improved" this question before including it in the Bible study, this will be a worthy challenge for me. But before I take a whack at improving this question, it's good to remember, again, that the best critical-thinking discussion questions are always surprising, specific, and personal. Let me explain.

- *Surprising* means you include something in the question that would take most people off guard. One way to do that is to take a random object—any little trinket sitting on your desk, for example—and use it as the spark for a surprising question about Jesus.

- *Specific* means you narrow the question from a broad focus to a very narrow focus. Your question should address only one well-defined target. So many bad questions are really two questions in one, so stick to one question per question, please.

- *Personal* means the question includes something that requires a personal response, not a theoretical response. It requires people to share out of their heart, not just their head.

Now, how can I make my test question better reflect Jesus' standards? I noticed a yellow highlighter sitting on my desk, so I came up with this: "Let's say you open your Bible in the morning and find that God has used his yellow highlighter to mark every place that references Jesus' sacrifice on the cross; why might he do that to your Bible?" Surprising, specific, and personal.

Awhile back, a friend asked me for help in pursuing the heart of a teenage girl she's mentoring in the foster-care system. My friend's normal, conventional approach to engaging young people—off-the-cuff questions that most often require only a yes-or-no answer—was failing. Their times together were dominated by awkward silences. My friend was afraid she wasn't cut out for this mentoring commitment. Here's the note she wrote me:

> "I recently started mentoring a 16-year-old girl. She is really quiet, really sweet. We have done some "activities" together—group volleyball, took her to Extreme Community Makeover on Saturday, and so on. But when I have just taken her out for ice cream or a picnic, there have been some quiet moments. I know her "file"—she's living in a foster home and her foster mother is trying to adopt her and they have a good relationship. The foster mom has shared some with me, too. She's been in foster care since she was 9, and in this home for three years. I know some about her biological parents—she's not seen two younger siblings since she was 9. She has never talked about any of this to me (I just know all of this from her file or her foster mom). Nor have I asked her about it; she's young, she doesn't know me. She sees a therapist; it's all pretty heavy and I'm not a therapist! I guess I'm looking for some "safe" but nevertheless thought-provoking, somewhat probing topics to discuss. I was hoping you might have guidance for me as I go into these unchartered, out-of-my-comfort-zone waters!"

I could see that my friend's heart for this girl was "all-in," but she felt lost in her pursuit of her. I offered her some surprising, specific, and personal alternative conversation-starters:

- Some people would love to win the lottery because they think that would solve all their problems; what do you think would "solve all your problems"? Why?

- What's something about yourself that you secretly admire, and why?

- What qualities are common threads that run through your friends? Why are you drawn to the friends you have?

- When you're really troubled or worried, what helps you feel at peace again? Explain why that's true for you.

Pursuing teenagers using surprising, specific, and personal questions feels like riding a bike for the first time. When we're first learning to do it, we tend to overthink the "filters" and stumble around. But the more we practice, the more we can stop overthinking our questions and have fun with them. How do I know? We've now trained thousands of youth workers to master it in less than 20 minutes at events all over the country. This quick exercise, practiced over and over, will quickly improve the quality and potency of your questions about Jesus.

When we ask better questions about Jesus, we create better

conversations about him. That's why I've created a question-practice that you can use for any teaching situation in your ministry. It's called the "Three-Question Strategy."

The Three-Question Strategy

You can use this simple-but-dynamic learning strategy whenever you're studying or teaching a Scripture passage that includes things Jesus said and did. First, choose a passage that's rich in "targets"—one packed with examples of Jesus engaging people. Then make three small signs with the following written on them:

1. "What did Jesus really say?" (Think of the context.)

2. "What did Jesus really do?" (What impact did his actions have?)

3. "How did people really experience Jesus?" (Look for emotional reactions.)

Post the three signs in three corners of your meeting room, and put a pile of Bibles under each sign. Then form trios. (It's very important that each small group has only three people in it; you'll understand why in just a moment.) Have trios decide which person in their group will go to each of the three corners and then split up and go to their assigned corner. Once they get to their corner, they should find a partner, open a Bible to the passage you're exploring, and work together to answer only their corner question.

Give them four or five minutes to explore their passage,

answer their question, and write their observations. Then ask them to return to their original trio and share what they discovered in their corner discussion. After five or 10 minutes, gather everyone together and ask your "essential question," the question you're asking all the time, in every circumstance, forever: "Who do you say Jesus is?" Encourage your students to always begin their answer to this question with "Jesus is...."

Keep your signs posted in the three corners, permanently. That way, you can use the three-question strategy at any time. It's a terrific way to create a "pursuit mentality" in your group, and it has a profound impact on your kids' learning takeaway. Here's why: In any learning situation, who in the room is learning the most? That's right, it's always the teacher. And in this three-question strategy, you're creating a roomful of teachers. Your students are pursuing Jesus with a partner, then sharing with their trio everything they learned. They're teaching, and they don't even know it. And they're learning to pursue Jesus with the sort of persistence that unlocks him.

Jesus taught his disciples about the power of persistent pursuit: "Imagine what would happen if you went to a friend in the middle of the night and said, 'Friend, lend me three loaves of bread. An old friend traveling through just showed up, and I don't have a thing on hand.' The friend answers from his bed, 'Don't bother me. The door's locked; my children are all down for the night; I can't get up to give you anything.' But let me tell you, even if he won't get up because he's a friend, if you stand your ground, knocking and waking all the neighbors, he'll finally get up and get you whatever you need" (Luke 11:5-8, THE MESSAGE). "Shameless persistence" is forceful and leveraging and bold. It compels the "friend" to open his door and "give you whatever you need." And when students are always knocking on Jesus' door, they end up getting to know him intimately. Pursuing others by persistently asking them questions isn't what Jesus would do; *it's what Jesus does.*

Communicating in R.E.A.L. Ways
By Thom and Joani Schultz

What do people mean when they call someone a "great communicator"? Generally, they mean the person delivers polished lectures, keeps an audience's attention for a period of time, and often hears "I really enjoyed your talk." A "great communicator" is an entertainer. And entertainment is a nice thing. Great communicators are nice to have around. A good lecture is more pleasant than a boring one. But is entertainment the goal of a Jesus-centered youth ministry? Did the impact and lasting effectiveness of Jesus' ministry hinge on a reputation akin to today's definition of a "great communicator"?

We think not. In fact, we're concerned that much of the youth ministry world has been sold a lie, with all good intentions. Many youth workers look longingly at the higher profile of their senior pastors and somehow conclude that ministry success looks like a riveting speaker enthralling an adoring but passive audience.

But that's not Jesus-centered ministry.

That's a ministry model borrowed from the entertainment world and the academic world. In the centuries following Jesus' ministry, the keepers of the church began to view faith as a subject to be mastered, much like any other subject such as literature or history. So, the thinking went, if we have a subject to teach, we need a studious professor and rows of passive students to hear the fact-filled lectures.

The trouble is, faith in Jesus isn't a subject to be mastered. Faith is a relationship, not an academic subject or a show. The nurture of this relationship looks a lot more like a friendship than a history class or a stage presentation. The goal of a great relationship is not the accumulation of factual knowledge or the applause of an entertained crowd. The goal of a great relationship is an ever-deepening love, trust, and commitment to one another that demonstrates itself through self-sacrifice.

Jesus didn't come to earth to be a "great communicator." He came to nurture life's most important relationship. He did that through many different ways. He sometimes communicated truths in front of a crowd. He also mentored one to one, asked lots of questions, led a small group, told stories, used visual aids, and led his people through highly memorable experiences in order to cement the relationship.

So, what can we learn about communicating in a Jesus-centered youth ministry? That communication, if it is to be truly effective and life-changing, must be R.E.A.L. That is, it must be Relational, Experiential, Applicable, and Learner-based:

- *Relational*. Communication (and relationship) is greatly enhanced when everyone gets to talk. And great questions fuel great conversations.

- *Experiential*. People learn—and change—by doing. Jesus knew this. That's why he used so many memorable experiences: washing the disciples' feet, calming a storm, mixing spit in the dirt to make a healing mud, and so on.

- *Applicable.* Effective communication in a Jesus-centered youth ministry isn't about information. It's about transformation. So our communication needs to center around real life. Students should leave with a clear idea of how a truth fits into their everyday life.

- *Learner-based.* It's not about you. It's about your students—and their relationship with Jesus. It doesn't matter how you were taught, how you like to learn, or how you're comfortable teaching. It's not about you. Just as Jesus did, we need to adapt our approach to most effectively reach our students.

Effective communication in ministry—and in a great relationship—has little to do with becoming a skilled entertainer or a know-it-all professor. Effective communication in ministry looks a lot like the kinds of communicating found in a healthy friendship.

—*Thom Schultz is Founder and CEO of Group Publishing.*

—*Joani Schultz is Chief Creative Officer of Group Publishing.*

IN PRACTICE

Question Strategies

Most adults are terrible question-askers. That's largely because the art hasn't been modeled for us. Generally, our teachers haven't asked us questions; they've lectured. Our coaches haven't asked us questions; they've directed and corrected. Our parents haven't asked us questions; they've exhorted. Our bosses haven't asked us questions; they've assessed our progress and handed out projects. So it's no wonder that so many of us stink at what Rick is urging us to do.

I'm trying to learn what he already excels at doing—asking great questions. But it hasn't been easy, because we pay so little attention to the "mechanics" of the art. What Rick just shared is the best practical stuff I've ever read on the topic, but here are two tiny tips that have helped us create a richer "inquiry-based" environment:

- We try to listen more than we talk. Asking good questions almost always goes hand in hand with being a good listener. We train our youth leadership team to "have big ears and a small mouth."

- We welcome questions ourselves. Part of creating a culture where your students respond well to question-asking is to allow them to ask questions! It's not always convenient or comfortable, but we strive to create an environment (especially in our small groups) where students can ask lots and lots of questions.

—Kurt Johnston

CHAPTER ELEVEN

THE JESUS PUSH-BACK

"He is the playfulness of creation, scandal and utter goodness, the generosity of the ocean and the ferocity of a thunderstorm; he is cunning as a snake and gentle as a whisper; the gladness of sunshine and the humility of a thirty-mile walk by foot on a dirt road." —John Eldredge

Because false beliefs about Jesus are keeping teenagers from loving him with all their heart, soul, mind, and strength, we must help them learn how to expose and undermine these misconceptions that are "wolves in sheep clothing." We live in a lazy-thinking culture. All of us, students and adults alike, have learned to soak in false "truths" and misleading assumptions about Jesus with little or no push-back. But no "truth" is true until we've explored it using a biblical filter. So we train kids to do what Jesus did when Satan tempted him in the wilderness; every time his enemy threw a lie at him, cloaked as a truth, Jesus pushed back with a biblical truth. And whenever he encountered a "conventional cultural truth" that contradicted the "norms" of the kingdom of God, Jesus pushed back using this repeated refrain: "You have heard it said, but I say...."

Jesus is the final word on all truth. And, more specifically, he's the final word on himself.

In a culture that elevates muscle fitness to a near-religion, the "muscle" most in need of strengthening is the one that fuels our critical thinking. Pastor and author John Ortberg says: "In the Gospel of Mark, the scribes asked Jesus, 'Which commandment is the most important of all?' And Jesus quotes from Deuteronomy 6:5—'You shall love the Lord your God with all your heart and with all your soul and with all your might'—but added the admonition to love God 'with all your mind.' Why the addition? Cornelius Plantinga called this the Magna Carta for the Christian intellectual life. To love God with all our minds means we should think about Him a lot—be interested in Him."[41]

Contrary to popular assumptions about followers of Christ (and sometimes supported by our "mindless" statements and simplistic responses to complex questions), Jesus isn't an anti-intellectual. In fact, he's challenged us to maximize our minds in our pursuit of him, and in the way we live our lives for him. Steve Case, a longtime youth minister and a contributing editor for Group Magazine, uses his extensive collection of "Jesus junk"—action figures and posters and night lights—to spark critical thinking in kids. For example, he has a 12-inch hot-pink Jesus figure that works like a Magic 8 Ball. You ask him a question and then turn him over to see an answer, such as "Let me ask my father," on the little floating triangle. Steve uses these junky items to teach his teenagers to see the irony underlying the typically lazy ways we think of Jesus. When teenagers learn to laugh at the ridiculous Jesus embedded in our culture's popular thinking—to throw intellectual stones at that false idol—they're simultaneously drawing near to him as he really is.

Vintage Church, the same congregation that produced the campy and ironic "Jesus Films" as a way to deconstruct the false Jesus of popular misconception, took the idea one step further. They created their own eight-episode sitcom called *The Believer Way*. It's designed to expose our lazy thinking and sharpen our ability to push back against false beliefs about Jesus and the Christian life. Here's how the ministry leaders who created this sitcom explain their mission:

> "[We] spent ten weeks in the book of Hebrews. It was clear the recipients of this letter were good-hearted, but a bit confused. You see, while they followed Jesus, they also questioned whether or not there needed to be something else added to the equation: angels, Jewish tradition, the Prophets, and more. This might seem like a foolish mistake, but we're still guilty of it today, with things such as small-group Bible studies, "quiet times," and Christian paraphernalia. While all of these things can be valuable, and often help us follow God, we need to be careful not to let them get in the way of what's most important: Jesus Christ. The sincere characters of our satirical sitcom *The Believer Way* struggle to follow God with their hearts, but often end up following tradition and religion instead."[42]

It's telling that the "stuff" that encircles our relationship with Jesus can be so quickly elevated above him. It's human nature, because our sin-damaged nature craves the worship of lesser gods. False versions of Jesus thrive because the real Jesus is often hard to stomach, let alone worship. The documentary *The Armstrong Lie* explores the Lance Armstrong doping scandal from an unusual perspective; it's less interested in the well-publicized ways the seven-time Tour de France winner lied about using performance-enhancing drugs to dominate the cycling world and more interested in the way so many people have steadfastly refused to accept the bitter truth about him. It's a film about our relentless pursuit of lesser gods. And we prefer lesser gods to Jesus.

Every day we're served up new evidence that proves this hard reality. In the aftermath of Nelson Mandela's funeral, for example, a young South African spoken-word artist named Thabiso Mohare wrote a poem in honor of the great anti-apartheid leader. Here's a portion of "An Ordinary Man":

> *And we watched the world weep*
> *For a giant bigger than myths*
> *A life owned by many*
> *Now free as the gods*

"Worshipful" is the best way to describe the tone that infuses this poem and all the other tributes that framed Mandela's death and funeral. And people give themselves over to this feeling because it's easier and more acceptable to worship Nelson Mandela (or Mother Teresa or Steve Jobs or Justin Bieber or Oprah Winfrey) than it is to worship the "Scandalon" who is Jesus. He alone is worthy to be worshipped, but not because we're "supposed to." Everything Jesus said and did fits together into a perfect mirror of the God we can't see but long to know. And the image of God we see in Jesus will bowl us over and transform us, if we'll only pay attention well enough to push back against what is false about him.

A Beautiful Mind

At the beginning of my oldest daughter's last year in middle school, my wife and I went to her back-to-school night. We followed a virtual trail of breadcrumbs through a cold gauntlet of lockers into the classroom jungle, and in our journey of seven classrooms, we spent 15 minutes with each of her teachers. It was a micro-taste of what Lucy's school day was like, along with a quick overview of what each teacher was planning to do over the next nine months. Our last stop was in her social studies class. Lucy had already told us she was nervous about this teacher, so we were expecting to be underwhelmed.

But we were wrong.

Her social studies teacher, it turns out, was quirky/passionate about teaching middle schoolers. His obsession was helping kids learn how to think critically. The topics he planned to target seemed almost secondary to him; his real goal was to entice young adolescents into thinking and doubting and exploring and pursuing. This, of course, must have sounded a little intimidating for Lucy—thus the ambivalence. But the more this guy described his teaching techniques, the better I liked him.

Two weeks later, that teacher abruptly resigned. He was near retirement and apparently was trying to hold out for one last year while laboring under an ominous medical diagnosis. But he couldn't do it. And after Lucy came home from school and told us the news, I was surprised by how deeply sad I felt—not just for the struggle this servant-teacher was facing but for the valuable training my daughter would now miss. Critical thinking is really the key to so many doors in life, and in youth ministry, it's a primary conduit for Jesus-centered discipleship.

Our conventional models for discipleship training—almost always some version of an "information download" seasoned with a video or a story—are fatally flawed, in much the same way our conventional models for public education are fatally flawed. I heard this fatal flaw threaded through an investigative report on why fewer than half of all Colorado students score at grade level in science, and most lose interest in it by fourth grade. Replace "science" with "biblical truth" in public radio reporter Jenny Brundin's report, and the impact is prophetic in scale:

> **Brundin:** When you explore the gargantuan question of why so many kids are failing in science, you find some of the answers just by talking to high school junior Elizabeth Ramsey.

Ramsey: A lot of us did not enjoy science class during middle school, and it kind of carried through with us here. Either they [teachers] just talked at us and we didn't really do anything—or we took the occasional note and listened. Others didn't do a really good job at explaining. We couldn't understand what they were saying, and they couldn't explain themselves very well.

Brundin: So what's going on in classrooms? Lots of talk about facts and procedures. And students mostly just listen. They don't get their hands on things, or they're often not required to figure things out on their own—that's according to a National Research Council study of high school science classrooms. [The key is] getting kids to think critically and invent, using real-world examples. Dissecting a frog or mixing chemicals in a beaker isn't enough. Research shows those lab exercises are more like following a recipe than discovering scientific principles. Here's Barry Cartright, former science specialist with the state Department of Education.

Cartright: Recent research has found that the method of delivery isn't as important as making sure the kids are really engaged in the material and having to do some deep thinking about it.

Brundin: That means "minds-on" instead of just "hands-on." They have to be mentally engaged. And that means asking questions, debating ideas, and gathering evidence to refine those ideas. The teacher guides the discussion and discovery. She asks challenging and reflective questions. Students who discover the answers will remember them much better than if a teacher told them in a lecture. Here's teacher Trish Loeblein's advice.

Loeblein: Try to figure out how to get the teacher out of the center stage and how to get the students realizing that they're the learners and that they need to be the doers.[43]

If our goal is for kids to discover the truth about Jesus and what it means to follow him, we'll need to find more ways to help them think critically about the "self-evident truths" they hear repeated over and over in their culture.

You Have Heard It Said...

The practice I call "The Jesus Push-Back" is a critical-thinking skill that will help students get inside the skin of Jesus—to think like he thinks about the influences that are exerting leverage on them. In it, we simply use the framework Jesus has already given us—"You have heard it said... but I say..."—to compare and contrast the common beliefs and conventional wisdoms of our culture. To start, we have to drag commonly accepted "truths" in our culture into the light, then match them with a kingdom-of-God truth that Jesus revealed.

Let's try this with a few sampler "truths" that match up well with the Beatitudes.

You have heard it said...	But I say...
• The weak and unsuccessful in life are modern-day lepers; they aren't people we want to hang around.	• "Blessed are the poor in spirit, for theirs is the kingdom of heaven."
• Never let them see you cry.	• "Blessed are those who mourn, for they shall be comforted."
• If you want to succeed in life, you'll need to push your way to the top.	• "Blessed are the meek, for they will inherit the earth."
• Do whatever makes you happy and you'll find fulfillment.	• "Blessed are those who hunger and thirst for righteousness, for they will be filled."
• The only way people will respect you is if they know they'll get hurt if they mess with you.	• "Blessed are the merciful, for they will receive mercy."
• Students who are "sheltered" from gritty cultural influences are missing out.	• "Blessed are the pure in heart, for they will see God."

- The goal is to win, not to make friends.

- "Blessed are the peacemakers, for they will be called sons of God."

- Don't get labeled a "goody-goody" at school; no one will want to hang out with you.

- "Blessed are those who are persecuted because of righteousness, for theirs is the kingdom of heaven."

- The worst thing in the world is to be the target of false rumors and accusations.

- "Blessed are you when people insult you, persecute you and falsely say all kinds of evil against you because of me. Rejoice and be glad, because great is your reward in heaven, for in the same way they persecuted the prophets who were before you."

When teenagers practice this "You have heard it said...but I say..." rhythm often enough, we turn on a switch in them that can't be turned off—ever. They learn to think through a permanent filter we've helped construct for them. It's called "holy skepticism." When they're operating in it, they accept no "conventional truths" that contradict the truths Jesus revealed. They learn to think like him in every circumstance, because they're discovering how countercultural he was in his thinking.

Embedding `Problem Time´

Another simple way to exercise your students' critical-thinking muscle and get them digging deeper into Jesus is to include a regular "Problem Time" segment in your weekly gatherings or your road trips or even your fun outings. Here's how it works: Develop a list of biblical problems connected to Jesus that need a solution. These are conundrums that we can't make sense of, or things Jesus did that seem counterintuitive, or stuff he said that makes us scratch our head. For example:

- Why did Jesus treat the beggar woman in Matthew 15 so harshly?

- Why, in John 7, did Jesus tell his brothers he wouldn't attend a feast in Judea, then later go anyway?

- Why, in John 6, did Jesus respond to the crowd's demand for greater clarity relative to his "Eat my body and drink my blood" proclamation by simply repeating himself, over and over?

- Why did Jesus choose to heal the man born blind by spitting in the dirt, making a mud pack, then smearing it on the man's face and forcing him to walk through town to wash in a pool?

- Why did Jesus choose Judas as a disciple?

- Why did Jesus tell Peter in advance that he would deny him?

We could go on and on here. The idea is to identify and list all the "Jesus problems" you can come up with, and then ask your group (in whatever setting you're in) to wrestle with one and come up with some possible solutions. Simply sprinkle these problems into your regular events and activities—even load them up on separate PowerPoint or MediaShout or ProPresenter slides so you can flash them onto a screen any time you want.

Teenagers already have what we might call a "garbage meter" hard-wired into their emotional circuit board, but these Jesus push-back practices will expand that meter's scope and purpose. The result is a high-torque relationship with him, where his perspective is a vital part of everyday life.

The Rebel Jesus
By Greg Stier

Years ago when I was a preaching pastor in Denver, Colorado, I used to go to the same restaurant every day to study for my sermons. I'd tank up on caffeine and the Spirit of God while hammering out my outlines and illustrations for the upcoming weekend services. One day after a few hours of studying, I gathered my Bible and books, picked up my coffee-stained bill, and took my place in line to pay. As I stood there, I felt somebody's eyes boring a hole through me. I turned to see a teenager staring at me with angry, hate-filled eyes. He looked about 16 years old; he was dressed completely in black, was covered in piercings, and had a snarl tattooed on his smirking face.

At first I didn't know what was going on, but then it hit me: This kid had been reading the words on the spines of the books tucked under my right arm. These were "Jesus books," and I could tell by the blaze in his gaze that this kid had a problem with that. When our eyes met, the situation got even more uncomfortable. The awkward moment led to his inevitable question, "Hey man, are you religious?"

I thought for a second and uttered, "I can't stand religious people. They make me want to puke."

"I can't stand them either!" he almost yelled. "They think they're better than everybody else!"

"Do you know who else couldn't stand them?" I asked.

"Who?" he answered.

"Jesus!" I shot back.

He looked surprised by my answer. "Are you serious?" he asked.

"I'm dead serious." I continued, "As a matter of fact, Jesus, the Son of God, came down from heaven to hang out with sinners like you and me, but the religious people got mad so they crucified him." Now this kid started to get real worked up that the religious people crucified Jesus.

So I went on: "But Jesus had the last laugh. Three days later he rose again from the dead, proving that he was God. Now he offers sinners like you and me eternal life if we simply trust in him." By the time I was finished, this kid raised his fist into the air and shouted something like, "Jesus is awesome!"

For the first time in his young life, this counterculture teenager encountered the real, relevant, nonreligious, counterculture Jesus. It took just a few minutes to blow his lame mental image of the Son of God to tiny bits of stained-glass shrapnel. We must do the same thing in our youth groups. Too many of our teenagers have never encountered the actual Jesus of the Bible. Too often their mental stereotype is the 6-foot-2, skinny-white-guy Jesus who loved peace, hated conflict, and did miracles. But the Jesus of the Bible would be far too intense for the average church today.

Building Jesus-centered evangelism into your youth ministry DNA means confronting teenagers with the Jesus they don't expect. The same Jesus who preached about heaven preached about hell even more. He is Savior and judge, lion and lamb, compassion and intensity.

We must use the same bold, beautiful, catalytic, and contentious colors that the Gospel writers used to paint him. When we do, maybe our kids will thrust their fists into the air and for the first time proclaim, "Jesus is awesome!"

—*Greg Stier is Founder and President of Dare 2 Share Ministries.*

IN PRACTICE

The Jesus Push-Back

"God's Way" and "World's Way." For years, these two signs have been posted on opposite sides of our high school room. And nobody used these signs more artfully, or more effectively, in our ministry than Doug Fields (my predecessor at Saddleback). In the middle of most lessons, Doug would, at just the right moment, move from one sign to the other, reminding our teenagers that every challenge we face in life can be approached "God's Way" or the "World's Way," and the two are almost always mutually exclusive.

Today, the signs aren't always posted in our room, but the tactic remains entrenched in the way we try to help our students navigate their world. The premise is simple: We don't want our students to drink the Kool-Aid of the world's way. We want them to be skeptics of the way their culture "naturally" thinks. Here's how we try to help them:

- **The Signs**—We do post our "God's Way" and "World's Way" signs when our teaching topics give us a natural fit. The signs provide a great excuse to remind our students to live with purpose, not simply give in to the flow of their culture.

- **The Flip**—We like to point out how often Jesus flipped conventional thinking on its ear and countered the "norms" of his culture with surprising truths.

- **The Crises**—This is a biggie. We don't protect our students from their crises of faith; in fact, we welcome them when they show up! Why? Because crises of faith require our teenagers to ask tough questions and to think critically about what they believe.

Many youth workers, and even more parents, actually discourage their teenagers from thinking critically, because they fear it will surface faith questions they can't answer. And they're right—it does. But that's a really good thing!

—*Kurt Johnston*

CHAPTER TWELVE

USE PARABLES

"One can tell oneself stories but not parables. One cannot really do so just as one cannot really beat oneself at chess or fool oneself completely with a riddle one has just invented. It takes two to parable." —John Dominic Crossan

A parable is a story that has a truth locked up in it. And that truth will remain locked unless we pay attention to the parable, search for its key, and open it. Jesus speaks in parables because he wants us to experience who he is and what life is like in his "native country"—which the Bible calls the kingdom of God—not just listen to static explanations of him. Just as any sojourner from a foreign land would do, Jesus has humbled himself to "speak our language," but he also wants us to learn what is native to him, and he uses parables to help us.

Because God has embedded our world with an extravagance of parables (nature-based "stories" with a truth locked up in them) and because Jesus spoke in parable so often (he told 55 parables in the Gospels), we can assume that parables are a focal point for translating God's native language. Jesus used them far more than what we might call "principles" or "tips and techniques" to teach. Why? He didn't suddenly start telling parables, or stories with truth at the center, as a novelty approach to teaching. The Trinity has always spoken the language of parable.

The difference between telling students principles and truths they should embrace and introducing them to the language of parable is the difference between me merely describing what's in the center of a delicious Reese's Peanut Butter Cup and inviting you to actually bite into one. For example, rather than merely urging us to take risks because risk is native to the kingdom of God, Jesus tells the parable of the talents. He draws us inside a compelling story, then asks us to find the treasure buried there. And that treasure is this: Jesus expects us to reflect his character and personality by taking risks on behalf of him.

So God is the one who has infused our world, the very air we breathe, with parable. He is the Headwaters of parable; every story that reflects the values and truths of the kingdom of God has its source in him. There is no truth that did not originate in him. And even though sin has marked us, we are made in God's image—all of us. So when we create something, we are acting like God and reflecting his nature. Every created thing, including those things we mistakenly suppose we've created in isolation, is actually created in partnership with the God of Parables. If we pay attention to creation—every created thing or every creative process—we find parables embedded in them. And, even more remarkable, this is true not just for people who've committed their lives to Jesus and have been reborn. It's true for everyone who bears his image. When Jesus entered Jerusalem on his way to the cross, and the people were worshipping him as the Messiah, the Pharisees demanded that this blasphemy stop. But Jesus responded:

"If these become silent, the stones will cry out" (Luke 19:40, NASB). Jesus will be worshipped, even if it emanates from those who are ignorant of him or think they have nothing to do with him.

Our calling as followers of Jesus and ministry leaders is to notice God—his attributes, power, and nature that are laid thick in the everyday "creation" experiences of our lives. We come to know him and "abide" in him by learning to notice him speaking to us in parable. If we pay closer attention not only to the parables Jesus left us but also to the beauty that captures us, the stories that engage us, and the truths that speak to us, we will come to know him more intimately.

The Parable Exercises

There are many creative ways to make the pursuit and experience of parables a staple in your ministry. I'll offer up some possibilities here. When you make these practices a part of your "norm" in ministry, you are speaking in Jesus' native tongue. You are helping students learn to unlock the kingdom-of-God truths Jesus has buried, like treasure, all around them. And those truths all point back to his essence.

1. Pursuing Jesus' Parables

Jesus told so many parables—some tiny and some epic—that we have plenty of possibilities to pursue. In general, his parables can be divided into two basic "species." The first is oriented toward revealing the "norms" of the kingdom of God. The second is focused on revealing the character and personality of God. You can use either species as a launching pad for coming to know Jesus more intimately. Use the first species to ask your students: "What is the kingdom of God like?" Use the second to ask them: "What is God like?" In small groups or all together, choose a parable to pursue, from either category, then have kids read it and answer the "macro" question attached to it ("What is the kingdom of God like?" or "What is God like?"). Here's a sampler list of parables that fit into both categories:

The kingdom of God is like...

- Parable of Wheat and Weeds—Matthew 13:24-30 (God is more concerned about growing wheat than pulling weeds.)

- Parable of the Pine Nut (or Mustard Seed)—Matthew 13:31-32 (What seems small can grow huge. Strength is nurtured over time.)

- Parable of the Yeast—Matthew 13:33 (A small addition makes a big difference.)

God is like...

- Parable of the Great Physician—Matthew 9:10-13 (He is a healer and inviter of the outsider.)

- Parable of the Moneylender—Luke 7:40-47 (He is an appreciator of the desperate and indebted.)

- Parable of the Lost Sheep—Luke 15:3-7 (He is a pursuer of lost valuables; and he's a partier.)

- Parable of the Treasure in the Field—Matthew 13:44 (Treasure belongs to those who appreciate it.)

- Parable of the Pearl of Great Price—Matthew 13:45-46 (Good things come to those who know treasure when they see it.)

- Parable of the Big Fishing Net—Matthew 13:47-50 (The redeemed and unredeemed are allowed to grow together. It's not obvious which is good and bad.)

- Parable of the Lost Coin—Luke 15:8-10 (He is diligent, and he won't give up until he finds what he's looking for.)

- Parable of the Prodigal Son—Luke 15:11-32 (He is forgiving, passionate, just, noncontrolling, full of grace and truth, and firm; he sees the heart and celebrates repentance.)

2. Unlocking Parables From Created Things

Remember the startling truth Paul revealed in Romans 1:20 (NASB): "Since the creation of the world His invisible attributes, His eternal power and divine nature, have been clearly seen, being understood through what has been made." If you have access to God's creation, no matter how minimal the access, you can help your students learn how to extract parable truths from whatever they find. Simply bring in samples (flowers, rocks, pine cones, plants, leaves, whatever), or have kids go outside and find anything from God's creation that they can bring back to your gathering place. Ask them to study their object in silence while asking this question of God: "What does this show me about your 'power, nature, or attributes'?" Then have them wait in silence, while continuing to study their object. Encourage students to "receive" whatever comes to them in this silence. Then end the time of silence by asking them to share their insight with a partner, a small group, or the whole group. Make sure to ask the group to engage their insights with added detail or observation (this is the time for you to weigh in with your perspective as well).

If you regularly bring in samples of "creation" to study, you'll help your kids come awake to the parables that surround them in everyday life. And they'll learn bedrock truths about who Jesus is—his power, nature, and attributes.

3. Discovering Parables Embedded in Cultural Influences

For the better part of two decades, we've included media-based discussion-starters in Group Magazine; we've called that section "Ministry and Media." The idea is simple. We pay attention to the songs, TV shows, and films that fill up students' cultural landscape, looking for parables embedded in them. Then we ask leaders to show their students the segment that includes the video parable, or listen to the song, and then process the parable through Jesus-centered discussion questions. Some of these cultural snippets are what you might call "low-hanging fruit."

One example is the scene from the film version of C.S. Lewis' *The Lion, the Witch, and the Wardrobe* where Mr. and Mrs. Beaver describe Aslan (Jesus) to Lucy Pevensie, who's visiting Narnia for the first time. (Duffy Robbins described this scene in Chapter 5.) Have kids watch the scene, then ask them: In the Bible, how was Jesus "unsafe but good" to the people around him? How has Jesus been "unsafe but good" in your life?

Parables just like this one are buried in all the created entertainment your teenagers are ingesting right now. Not everything in these influences is a parable, of course, but God has shrewdly buried clues about himself in their culture. It's up to us to find them and use them to point kids back to who Jesus really is, and what living in his kingdom is really like. Jesus constantly mined parables from the culture of his day. Remember the parables of the laborers in the field, the weeds and the wheat, and the pearl of great price? Jesus drew these stories directly from his cultural influences. They were very familiar to people he was trying to teach. If we're awake to the parables that surround us, we can use them as door-openers to the deepest places in kids' hearts.

Here are a couple of parables extracted from popular culture for a recent issue of Group Magazine. You'll notice the simple structure of how they work. Anyone can create these parable discussion-starters, using almost anything teenagers are into.

A Parable From Music

Song: Switchfoot's "Let It Out" (from the album *Fading West*)

Theme: The singer is completely open about his faith and wants to just "let it out."

Scripture Focus: Matthew 5:14-16

Discussion Questions: Tell about a time you downplayed your beliefs to avoid embarrassment. What made you decide to do that? Tell about a time you stood firm with your faith, even when it was hard. Why did you speak out? What does Jesus mean when he describes us as the light of the world? How does shining our light reflect on Jesus? What's keeping you, right now, from "letting out" your faith more fully?

A Parable From a Film

Film: *Monsters University*

Theme: Identity

Scripture: Ephesians 2:10

Clip Location: 01:24:10 through 01:27:20 (DVD Chapter: 28)

Synopsis: Mike and Sully find themselves in the human world, being chased by police officers. It takes Mike convincing Sully to step into his true self to save them.

Gospel Filter: Teenagers (and adults) often doubt their abilities. If they could hear Jesus speaking the truth about who they really are, they could change the world.

Discussion Questions: What did Mike mean when he said, "Stop being a Sullivan and start being you!"? Describe a time you did something you were sure you couldn't do. What changed in you to make you think you could do it? Why do we doubt our own abilities so much? Read aloud Ephesians 2:10. How does it make you feel to be called God's masterpiece? When do you have a hard time accepting that title, and why? What are some of the "good things" Jesus has planted in you that others have benefited from?

4. Creating Experiential Parables

Another way to plunge students more deeply into Jesus' parables is to create experiences that mirror them. The idea is to capture the essence of a parable in a simple experience that plunges kids into doing, not merely hearing. Here's an example, using the parable of the good shepherd (John 10:1-5). Have your teenagers each find a partner; one person will be the Shepherd, the other will be the Sheep. Give a blindfold of some kind to each of the Sheep and have them put it on. Scatter the Shepherds around the room, each far away from their assigned Sheep. Then ask the blindfolded Sheep to find their way back to their Shepherd by only listening to his or her voice. Here's the catch: Shepherds can only call out "Sheep! Sheep!" to try to guide their Sheep back to them. Give them one minute to do this, and see how many are successful. Then have all the Sheep take their blindfolds off, find their Shepherd (if they haven't already), and discuss these questions: What made this activity hard for you? What makes it difficult for you in everyday life to recognize Jesus' voice?

The idea, again, is to create a simple parable experience that's tied to a Jesus-centered question. We plunge students into the parable experience, then connect the experience back to the parable with "beelined" discussion questions.

5. Mining Parables From Your Life

Here's a startling revelation: Jesus hasn't only planted parables in his creation, he's also planted them in your life's story. I mean, you've had experiences in your life that have parable-truths locked up in them. The sad truth is that we often fail to unlock those truths from our own lives because we're not paying close attention. But if you pay closer attention to the stories of your life—and the stories embedded in the lives of your students—you will find Jesus revealing himself through them. Here's how this works...

Think of a story from your life—anything that surfaces in your mind, or a story that's memorable because it impacted you (positively or negatively). (*Elevator music*) Now ask God in the silence: How might this story be a parable—something that reveals who you are, or what life is like in your kingdom? (*Elevator music*) What surfaces for you in the quiet? If you wait long enough, the parable-truth will emerge from your story.

For example, here's something I experienced that's memorable for me: I was driving down the highway during rush hour and saw a bunch of papers swirling around, getting chewed up in the traffic. I passed an off-ramp, where I saw a guy getting out of his car to grab the last few sheets of paper stuck on the back of his car. He'd obviously stacked his important papers on his car when he left home, then forgot they were there. I remember that story because I put myself in his shoes; it was heartbreaking. So I ask Jesus to show me the "parable connection" in this story. In other words, how can this story teach us something about who God is, or what life in God's kingdom is like? In my story, the parable connection Jesus revealed to me has to do with the consequences of my sin. I can be forgiven by him, but like that paper scattered all over the highway, I can't keep the effects of my sin from spreading. I can't take back the consequences.

This practice of mining parables from your life, or your students' lives, can be part of your everyday pursuit of Jesus. One popular retreat speaker has been doing this for years. She keeps a condensed list of her life parables with her and asks God to show her which stories to tell before every speaking engagement. She's constantly adding to the list. As you move through your daily experiences, ask Jesus to show you your parables. And teach your students to do the same.

Slaughtering a Sacred Cow

A mountain of research discounts lecturing as an effective way to help people learn, especially young people. But even if you're a big believer in sermons, I'm guessing you'd be hard-pressed to point to a sermon or message that actually changed your life. Life-change is almost always the result of an experience followed by some kind of Jesus-centered context for it. Though sermons are incredibly popular, they're not all that effective. So why do so many people continue to use them? Well, I asked youth leaders in our online community to tell me why, and they said:

- Sermons require less time, work, creativity, and risk.

- Youth talks are traditional in ministry—"that's how we were trained to teach, and we've always done it that way."

- There are (supposedly) few resources that help youth leaders teach in active and interactive ways (though this is the primary teaching strategy we embed in all our Group/SYM resources—simplyyouthministry.com).

- It's all an issue of control; "messages" keep the control in the youth leader's hands.

In our youth ministry training events, I often ask youth pastors to find a partner in the crowd and share about "something you've learned that has deeply impacted your life—something that turned your life around." They each get a couple of minutes to do it, and then I ask everyone to close their eyes. Next, I ask them to raise their hands if they primarily communicated their profound learning using principles, or if they did it by primarily telling a story. I've done this many times now, and I always find a 25/75 split in the crowd; 25 percent taught using principles and 75 percent taught using stories. In my experience, the percentages are exactly flipped in the church. Three-quarters of us primarily teach using principles; only a quarter (at best) primarily teach using stories. So when we don't realize we're "teaching," why do three-quarters of us naturally use story-parables instead of principles?

Because our hearts understand something our heads refuse to accept.

Experiences give us our deepest, longest-lasting lessons in life. That's why we're so fascinated by stories and why Jesus used parables and experiences to teach so often. In fact, his principle-to-story ratio was probably more like 20/80. People are riveted by parables, but they have to work to pay attention to principles. The Beatitudes in Matthew 5 were based on principles of truth; the parables throughout the Gospels were stories of truth. We experience the power behind story-based communicating every week. The next time you're listening to your pastor give a sermon, pay attention to the difference in the congregation when the pastor is teaching principles and when the pastor tells a real-life story. It's often rather noisy during principle time but incredibly quiet during story time.

Here's the truth: We greatly overuse principle-based teaching and greatly underuse parable-based teaching and experiences.

IN PRACTICE

Using Parables

Here's the condensed version of Storytelling 101—from a guy who's told his fair share of worthless stories.

- The only thing worse than no story in your lesson is a pointless story.

    The Practice: Never tell a story just for the fun of it. If it doesn't fit, don't force it into the lesson.

- Make the point of the story the point of the story!

    The Practice: You want students to remember the truth that the story points to, not merely the awesome story itself. Tell the story well, but tell the point of the story equally well.

- The payoff always needs to equal the setup.

    The Practice: The longer the story, the more powerful the point needs to be. If you're going to spend 10 minutes telling a story, it needs to pack a real punch!

- If you wouldn't tell the story with parents or your pastor in the room, don't tell it.

    The Practice: Sketchy, shocking, scandalous, and sexy stories usually backfire.

- Uphold your storytelling integrity.

  The Practice: Don't exaggerate. Don't tell made-up stories as if they were true. Don't tell others' stories as if they were your own.

—*Kurt Johnston*

CHAPTER THIRTEEN

HELP STUDENTS EMBRACE THEIR TRUE NAME

"Hello. My name is Inigo Montoya. You killed my father. Prepare to die." —Mandy Patinkin, from The Princess Bride

If you were born a Native American 200 years ago, or a Jew 2,000 years ago, the name you received from your parents wouldn't merely express their sensibilities and preferences; it would project onto you an identity your parents hoped you would live into. Your naming would be less of a label and more of a description; less of a nod to history and more of an act of faith and hope. That's because these cultures understood something that's true in the kingdom of God: The names we embrace in our life are the names we become.

We're now near the end of this journey, and so far we've exclusively explored practices that target only the first of two Core Questions extracted from Matthew 16: "Who do I say Jesus is?" But the second Core Question—"Who does Jesus say I am?"—is a crucial bookend. After the fisherman Simon "names" Jesus as Messiah, Jesus renames him Peter (*Petros*, which means "rock"). Jesus says, "I also say to you that you are Peter, and upon this rock I will build My church; and the gates of Hades will not overpower it" (Matthew 16:18, NASB).

In renaming his closest friend with a descriptive word that had never before been used as a name, Jesus answers two big questions for him: *Who am I?* and *What am I doing here?* The universal rhythm embedded here is both important and profound. As we name Jesus, he names us. And the name he gives us projects onto us an identity born out of his faith in us. In the church we often talk about our faith in God, but we rarely explore the biblical reality that Jesus has faith in us. He created in us an identity that's tied to a purpose in his kingdom, and our journey with him through life is a continuous revelation of that identity. He is bent on revealing our true identity that's tied to our true name in the kingdom.

But because the names we embrace are the names we become, our name is the chosen battleground for God's enemy in our life. We're caught in the middle of a war over our identity; in fact, every assault from hell on our life always has a component designed to destroy our God-given identity. If God's enemy can pollute or destroy what is most true about us, then we'll live out of a false identity and fuel his purposes in our life—and his purposes are to "steal, kill, and destroy." This is why it's so crucial for youth ministry leaders to help their students discover, embrace, and live out of their true identity in Christ—their true name. As we plant a grand pursuit in their life—"Who do I say Jesus is?—we simultaneously introduce a companion pursuit—"Who does Jesus say I am?"

The Aragorn Moment

As we more and more "name" Jesus for who he really is, he names us for who we really are. Jesus is so generous. He wants to reveal to us who we are and what we were made to do. One of the profound purposes of youth ministry is to create the right setting and circumstances for kids to experience Jesus unveiling them.

In *The Return of the King*, J.R.R. Tolkien's powerful conclusion to the *Lord of the Rings* saga, the man who's spent his life as a ranger, the man who calls himself Strider, must step into his true role as King of Gondor to lead the forces of good against the forces of evil. Because of the shame he feels over the cowardice of his ancestors, Aragorn has deftly avoided embracing his identity as king and continues to live by a nickname given to him by others—Strider. It's as if he's afraid to become what he was meant to be. But then a wise, older mentor calls him out.

In one of the film's climactic scenes, Aragorn is summoned to a tent where he finds a hooded figure, the elven Lord Elrond, waiting for him. He's there to challenge Aragorn to embrace his true identity because the fate of the world hangs on his leadership. Elrond hands Aragorn a sword called Anduril, a legendary weapon wielded by the great kings of Gondor. I'll let the film's screenplay pick up the story:

> **Aragorn:** (Takes the sword, staring at it in wonder.) Sauron will not have forgotten the sword of Elendil. (He draws the long blade from its sheath.) The blade that was broken shall return to Minas Tirith.
>
> **Elrond:** The man who can wield the power of this sword can summon to him an army more deadly

than any that walks this earth. (Elrond stares hard at Aragorn.) Put aside the Ranger—become who you were born to be—take the Dimholt Road. (A heavy silence hangs in the room.) [44]

Of course, in the story Aragorn goes on to assume the mantle of king and lead the forces of good to victory over Sauron and the forces of darkness. When I show this powerful scene to youth pastors who are learning how to shift their ministry to a Jesus-centered mentality, I ask them to pinpoint what Elrond says that forces a turning point in Aragorn's life. The answer: Elrond tells Aragorn who he really was and challenges him to step fully into his true identity—his true name. And here Tolkien is embedding a theological and biblical reality inside his epic story of sin and redemption.

Has God ever answered this overshadowing question in your life? I mean, when have you sensed him revealing to you who you really are?

I remember my "Aragorn moment" so well. It was a little over 10 years ago. I was speaking at a youth ministry conference— the last place I wanted to be at that moment in my life. My wife and I were in the throes of a significant challenge to our young marriage. I'd left for the speaking trip upset and worried; I could sense our relationship was in some danger, and it was killing me. I mean I literally felt like someone was repeatedly jamming a dagger into my gut. I walked through the halls of the convention center hoping no one would recognize me so I wouldn't have to talk with anyone. My interior conversation was full of accusations and criticisms—all directed at myself. My identity was under full-scale assault, and I was sinking fast.

It was during one of my wall-hugging walks down a crowded hallway that I felt God breaking through my defenses and helping me to understand better the emotions and thoughts running through my mind. God spoke to me like a lightning bolt. It seemed so clear that I had to step into an empty room and write it all down as the words came gushing at me. I couldn't have been more shocked (and named) by what I sensed. Here's what I wrote down:

> You're a quarterback. You see the field. You're squirming away from the rush to find space to release the ball. You never give up. You have courage in the face of ferocity—in fact, ferocity draws out your courage. You want to score even when the team is too far behind for it to matter. You love the thrill of creating a play in the huddle, under pressure, and spreading the ball around to everyone on the team. You have no greater feeling than throwing the ball hard to a spot and watching the receiver get to it without breaking stride. In fact, you love it most when the receiver is closely covered and it takes a perfect throw to get it to him. You have the same feeling when you throw a bomb and watch the receiver run under it, or when you tear away from the grasp of a defender, or when you see and feel blood on your elbows or knees and feel alive because of it. You love to score right after the other team has scored, but you want to do

it methodically, first down by first down, right down the field. You love fourth down! You want to win, but you're satisfied by fighting well.

Many years after this crisis in my life, God used its brutal leverage in my soul to unveil my true identity and bring radical and beautiful change in my marriage. Of course, "Quarterback" is just a metaphor for something much more pertinent and treasured: the true nature of my heart and identity. God was describing me as I really am, and he did it at a desperate moment in my life. Instead of fixing my problem, he revealed my true name. And as the years go by I yield, more and more, to my true identity. In so many ways, youth ministry leaders are the midwives in the birth (or rebirth) of a Jesus-centered identity in the lives of teenagers. Nothing you do in ministry will impact them more deeply or broadly, and it will bear fruit for their rest of their lives.

The Practice of Positive Labeling

I know "labeling" is politically incorrect and akin to a sin in our culture today, but God is calling us—as mentors and leaders who recruit and train mentors—to vigorously, passionately, positively label our students. Positive Labeling is the key to helping them hear from Jesus about who they really are. The point here isn't simply to become more affirming, though most affirmation isn't a bad thing, of course. Affirmation is designed to make someone feel good about who they are. The practice of Positive Labeling is designed to reveal to a person his or her true nature. The goal is to pay attention to what God is doing in your teenagers, identify it, and name it—to help them hear how Jesus describes them.

When you practice Positive Labeling with your kids, you'll learn to act like a detective in their life—like Sherlock Holmes looking for evidence of their "real name." You'll learn (and teach your adult leaders) to pay attention to and pounce on little details that reveal a God-given identity in your students. The goal is to solve the mystery of their purpose in God's kingdom—to set the stage for them to hear how God describes their true identity.

I created a simple worksheet to help energize this process. It's called The Sherlock Holmes File. You simply choose a teenager in your group you know pretty well and then answer a few simple questions about that young person. Try it right now. Plug a teenager's name into the worksheet and take a few minutes to fill it out (*see the form on the following page*).

The Sherlock Holmes File for...

1. Three things I've noticed that this person seems to love:

-

-

-

2. Three ways I've seen this person contribute:

-

-

-

3. One way I've experienced this person's strength and/or gifting:

4. When this person seems most alive, he/she is usually doing this:

5. One thing this person does that seems to come easily:

6. One way this person could likely serve in ministry:

7. Stop now to pray: "God, who do you say this person is?" Write what you sense or "hear."

8. Positive Label: On a regular basis, here's how I will "name" this person—what Jesus has revealed about him/her.

This is a very powerful process, so don't take it lightly. It's God who knows each of your teenagers' real names, and it's God who will reveal those names to each of them. In Isaiah 43:1 (NASB) God says: "Do not fear, for I have redeemed you; I have called you by name; you are Mine!" This isn't a process any of us should do alone. Choose the person on your team who knows each young person best, and have that person fill out this worksheet. If no one knows a teenager well enough to fill out a sheet, that's telling you something. It's time to pursue.

As your team fills out these sheets, get together to discuss what you've learned. When you're all doing this regularly and you commit to communicating their "true identity" in a multitude of ways, your students will be encouraged to consciously move toward who they really are and give what they have to give. This skill of Positive Labeling will infuse your mentoring with power, so make sure you train adult leaders in it. In fact, every single adult in your ministry should consider himself or herself Sherlock Holmes on a mission from God.

By the way, before you play with this idea, I suggest you fill out a Sherlock Holmes File for yourself and ask someone close to you to also fill it out for you. After both of you have filled out the sheet, compare what you've written. Then go to your favorite coffee shop, bakery, or hot wings emporium and discuss two simple questions: What do we notice about the similarities between our lists; what stands out, and why? What do we notice about the differences between our lists; what stands out, and why?

When kids start to feel subtly and consistently saturated with true messages about their Jesus-fueled identity, they'll start saying things like teenagers at Rochester Covenant Church in Rochester, Minnesota, do. Listen to the impact of Positive Labeling on these "exemplary youth ministry" kids:

- "Our leaders do a good job and really take the time to notice our gifts.... I've gone out for coffee and they say, 'I've noticed you're really gifted in these areas.' That means so much more that they took the time to notice."

- "They don't just assign us to something."

- "When they tell you you're good at something, you're not just a number in the youth group. They are thinking about you and praying for you daily."

These teenagers can actually articulate how well their adult leaders are helping them discover their true identity in Christ, and that practice sends a profound message to them: "You belong here, because we see you well." A community of teenagers who feel well-seen will naturally draw others into it.

Asking the Question

The forming power of embracing your true name is unmistakable and more saturating than we realize, and it's not hard to find examples of its impact. There are two middle-aged brothers in my church whose last name, for most of their lives, was literally "Failure." For years they labored through life, burdened by the latent curse of their surname and sometimes unconsciously obeying its prophetic gravity. Later in life, after their wives had begged them for years to change their name, the men decided to research the origins of "Failure" and discovered it's an Americanized version of their original German surname, Fehler. When they formally adopted the German original as their last name, it's as if the sun rose over their landscape. That's because the names we embrace are the names we become.

Is it possible that we all have two names—the one our parents gave us and the one God calls us when he's plotting his next adventure? And is it possible Jesus wouldn't mind if we asked him who we really are, and helped our teenagers do the same?

Author and pastor Walter Wangerin says there are, universally, two "creation" languages. The first is spoken by God, who "spoke everything into being" out of nothing at all. The second is the language God first gave to Adam, the language of naming (Genesis 2). Names, says Wangerin, are not merely labels: "The thing named is brought into place so it can be known. A name establishes a person's relationship with other named things. The naming action begins to declare the person's purpose. And this naming is powerful, but also dangerous."[45]

Naming, truly, is powerful and dangerous. Damning, accusing words or descriptions are, of course, not from God. Normal parents never describe the essence of their children with words that damn. Never. Your students already know what's wrong with them; they know their own list of deficits very well. But most of them know very little about the person God has described as "fearfully and wonderfully made" (Psalm 139:14). It's God who knows their real name, and it's God who can reveal it to them if he wants to. Remember this again, from Isaiah 43:1 (NASB): "Do not fear, for I have redeemed you; I have called you by name; you are Mine!" These are the sweetest words your teenagers will ever hear in life.

So in addition to acting like Sherlock Holmes in students' lives, helping them discover their true, God-given identity, we can also help them explore the answer to this life-changing Core Question: "Who does Jesus say I am?" Find a place to do this where teenagers can have some quiet space, where they can have a sense of safety and isolation. Retreats are a great setting to try this experiment. The key is to do this at a time when your students are naturally at a lower energy level and to make sure they have the physical and emotional space they need to feel "alone."

They'll need something to write on and with. Then, in the quiet, have them simply ask Jesus: "Who do you say I am?" Before they ask Jesus this question, instruct them to do two things: "Tell God you want him to silence your own voice, and then ask him to silence the voice of his enemy." Then have students sit quietly and ask Jesus the question: "Who do you say I am?" Have them write what they sense. Assure them they won't have to share any of this with others unless they want to. Remind them it's possible they may not hear anything from God at this time, and that's OK, too.

After they finish this activity, form small groups with at least one adult leader in each one. Ask those students who'd like to share about their experience to do so in their small group. Then make your adult leaders available for private, one-on-one connection times for kids who'd like to discuss the experience but don't want to do it in front of other teenagers. Whatever you learn about your teenagers should be shared with your whole leadership team, so all of you can support and undergird the revealed identities of your kids. By the way, it's a good idea for you and your volunteer leaders to do this before you ask your students to do it.

Teenagers are craving relationship with people who are all-in with them—who are pursuers by their very nature. They're drawn to people who will enter into their world like missionaries, not people who offer relationship only inside their own comfort zone. They're longing, like we are, to discover their true identity, and to find out if God cherishes and enjoys them. And we've been invited into that epic mission with them. We, like Jesus our Master, are called to "set captives free," and the primary captivity of God's children is their imprisonment inside a false identity. The names we embrace are the names we become.

The Wheat-and-Weeds Imperative

Marcus Buckingham and Donald O. Clifton, authors of the bestselling business book *Now Discover Your Strengths*, popularized a profound truth that applies to the skill of Positive Labeling. It's a truth that's locked up in a strange little story Jesus told, the Parable of the Weeds in Matthew 13:24-30....

> "The kingdom of heaven is like a man who sowed good seed in his field. But while everyone was sleeping, his enemy came and sowed weeds among the wheat, and went away. When the wheat sprouted and formed heads, then the weeds also appeared.
>
> "The owner's servants came to him and said, 'Sir, didn't you sow good seed in your field? Where then did the weeds come from?'
>
> " 'An enemy did this,' he replied.
>
> "The servants asked him, 'Do you want us to go and pull them up?'
>
> " 'No,' he answered, 'because while you are pulling the weeds, you may root up the wheat with them. Let both grow together until the harvest. At that time I will tell the harvesters: First collect the weeds and tie them in bundles to be burned; then gather the wheat and bring it into my barn.' "

Jesus is essentially saying, "Don't pay attention to the bad stuff—the weeds; instead, concentrate on nurturing the good stuff. I'll take care of the bad stuff later on." Buckingham and Clifton make the case that the best way to manage people is to discover their strengths and fuel them, not look for their weaknesses and try to remove or improve them. Companies that shift their attention from trying to attack their workers' weaknesses and instead concentrate on fueling their strengths experience remarkable success.[46]

Translated to youth ministry, this new skill means we look for the kingdom of God in our teenagers and then speak it out to them, habitually and regularly. We recognize their "weeds," but we concentrate on growing their "wheat" instead. We help kids discover who they are, not who they aren't.

Be-With Mentoring
By Bo Boshers

When I first started in youth ministry, we planned an outreach event every Tuesday night. After the program was over, the leadership team—a dozen high school and college kids—gathered in the parking lot by a low brick wall. At first a parade of young people who'd attended that night would file by to say hi and introduce their friends. Later, after everyone else had said goodnight, I'd be standing next to that wall with my five key leaders: Coleman, Dave, Troy, Trevor, and Alex. We were always the last to leave, patiently waiting for storytelling time to begin.

We told such a wide variety of stories, from funny to touching. We laughed about what went wrong that night, how bad the music was, mistakes in the drama, something I said in the message that didn't make sense, or something that happened during the sports competition. Then the mood changed and the stories shifted from the evening's activities to kids' changed lives. Maybe one of my leaders had been praying for months that a friend would come and that friend had finally shown up—and loved it. Or maybe another would talk about a Jesus-centered conversation with a teenager who was, for the first time, exploring a relationship with him. We had fantastic celebrations when we found out a student had prayed to receive Christ.

I remember looking at these young men, listening to their stories, and thinking: "This is what I want to give my life to.

This is what really matters to me." I felt incredibly fulfilled every time I looked into their eyes and saw their compassion, their commitment, and their love for God. Sitting on that brick wall, right there in an empty parking lot, God showed me what ministry was all about. I could put up with all the other "stuff" of youth ministry for that payoff. More than 25 years later, I still love "sitting on the brick wall," looking into the eyes of a few teenagers I know and love well and seeing their passion, their desire, their ambition to change the world.

Jesus was the catalyst for deep personal transformation in those who followed him. Hang around him long enough, and you'd find your life radically altered. Dallas Willard says, "Christians must be weighed, not just counted." The disciples were so altered by Jesus' life and teaching that they gave the rest of their natural lives to perpetuating his work. At the heart of any ministry that seeks to emulate Jesus must be a commitment from the leaders to mentor a few in the daily aspects of living. I call that the Be-With Factor. Jesus lived it, and it's God's call on everyone who follows in his steps. It means mentoring is by far the most rewarding activity for anyone who cares about young people. Whatever else you do, commit to "being with" a few so that lasting life change happens.

—*Bo Boshers is President of LEAD222, an international coaching and mentoring ministry.*

IN PRACTICE

Helping Students Embrace Their True Name

I think Rick saved the best for last! Nothing is more important in your youth worker job description than helping students understand their true identity in Jesus Christ. And because they're navigating a culture where parents, teachers, coaches, friends, movies, music, magazines, and so many others are always defining who they are on their terms, your role has never been tougher or more vital. These are the three things we do in our ministry to help students embrace their true name:

1. **Refuse to focus on the superficial.** Don't dwell on the stuff in your teenagers' lives that doesn't really matter, whether it's good stuff (he's the varsity quarterback) or bad stuff (she got grounded for poor grades). The surface pros and cons in a student's life have little (or nothing) to do with who they truly are.

2. **Catch teenagers in the act of reflecting Jesus.** How we act doesn't always reflect the real us—but it might. When you see students doing things that reflect the character of Jesus Christ, let them know!

3. **"Name" them, even when they can't name themselves.** Rick's story about sensing God naming him Quarterback is a profound example of the confidence that comes when God sees something in us

that we don't see (although I've seen Rick throw, and "Quarterback" might be a little sketchy—but I digress). Don't make stuff up, but please, please, please don't be afraid to share what you know God believes about your teenagers.

Remember, few others are helping the students in your youth group discover who they really are. Don't miss the opportunity!

—*Kurt Johnston*

A CLOSING IMPERATIVE

"DETERMINED TO KNOW NOTHING"

When I was a kid, I didn't have the following toys, gadgets, or devices:

- Video games
- Internet
- iPod
- iPhone
- Motorized scooter
- Game Boy
- Cell phone
- Personal computer
- Cable TV

Hard to believe, isn't it? And I'm merely in my early 50s.

The "electronic football" I played when I was a kid involved plugging in a little football field, arranging 11 little plastic men on plastic platforms on offense and defense, and then turning on the switch so the field emitted an electronic "buzz," thus moving the little plastic men randomly toward each other (or not). When I was really young, I played mostly with my G.I. Joe army men. But I did have what I considered a cutting-edge toy that gave my G.I. Joe adventures the spark they really needed: a magnifying glass.

Let's say my good-guy G.I. Joes were trapped inside a little twig building I'd constructed, and my bad-guy G.I. Joes had thrown some toilet paper inside the building (for some inexplicable reason). Then, shockingly, the bad guys hauled out a magnifying glass and used it to focus the sun's rays on all that toilet paper. Pretty soon, whoosh! Those good-guy G.I. Joes came rushing out of the burning building, where they were forced to engage in hand-to-hand combat with the bad guys (who bore a startling resemblance to the good guys).

To me, the magnifying glass had something like magical ability. I had only a bare idea of how it worked. Of course, it's curved slightly to form a convex lens. It bends the light rays from an object so it appears larger. And when it's placed between an object and direct sunlight, it bends all those light rays into a single point, making that point really, really hot.

Jesus-centered youth ministry is a lot like that magnifying glass. When we use Spurgeon's beeline as the "curved lens" for everything we do, and put it between Jesus and our kids, something flames up. In this case, we're not burning toilet paper; we're lighting a fire in our teenagers, our adult leaders, and ourselves. And this particular fire is a "consuming fire" which means we all end up consumed by and for Jesus.

That's a nice description of the Christian life in full: following Christ because you're consumed by him, because he's the hub of your wheel, because you're undeniably, unapologetically, aggressively Jesus-centered. We know the *National Study of Youth and Religion* finds that only 10 percent of us have a "hub" relationship with Jesus, so let's make sure we and the young people we're influencing are 10-percenters through and through.

Let's embrace the beeline.

After all, a "devoted faith" is really just the normal Christian life for those who've been ruined by Jesus and ruined for Jesus.

Imagine for a moment you're standing on a beach at the Sea of Tiberias. You've just lived through the most spectacular stretch of days in all of history, as Jesus has suffered, died, been buried, and then resurrected. You don't know, really, what to do with your life now, so you ask your friends if they'd like to go fishing. For one night you go back to the life you knew before the hurricane of Jesus swept through your life. So you fish all night, catching nothing. And in the morning, one of your friends sees a man on the beach, watching. He recognizes that man as Jesus, so even though you're stripped naked for your work, you leap over the side of the boat and thrash your way to the shore. You arrive dripping wet and full of expectation. You feel the warmth of the fire he's built, and you smell a good breakfast cooking over it. And you can't stop grinning because... it's Jesus. He's alive and smiling at you.

A couple of your friends are putting the fire out now, and you can smell the smoke. You glance over at Jesus and realize he's staring right at you... right through you. He asks you to take a little walk with him. So you get up, but you keep looking at him because your soul is buzzing. You're walking next to Jesus again. He turns, looks at you again, and asks a question that bites a little: "Do you truly love me more than any other?" A little startled, you tell him... What?

In response, Jesus says: "Feed my lambs." Then you walk a little farther in silence. This time he doesn't turn to you; his eyes are focused way down the beach. He asks again: "Do you truly love me?" And you respond... How?

Now Jesus stops and turns, his face uncomfortably close to yours. He won't take his eyes off you. "Take care of my sheep," he says. Then, leaning in slightly, he asks one more time, "Do you love me?" And you can't hide your hurt anymore. You tell him... What?

Jesus backs away slightly and looks at you with a mixture of tenderness and fierceness. Then you see a grin just dawn on his face as he says, one more time, with gravity, "Feed my sheep." There's a long pause now... You have time to ponder what it means to feed Jesus' sheep. Then Jesus starts walking again. He gets a few yards ahead of you and you see him glance back, then call you by a name you've never heard before, but it seems vaguely familiar. You look at him... he's smiling. You rush to catch up.

BONUS IDEAS

Saturation is the key to beelining your youth ministry—to shifting its focus from a tips-and-techniques mentality to a Jesus-centered passion. What might happen if we raised the waterline in our ministries by saturating our teenagers with the beeline to Jesus in even the most mundane, obscure things we do. For example:

- **Language**—What if we changed the way we talk with teenagers to communicate something true about Jesus all the time? I wrote a column for Group Magazine titled "Don't Be Safe." I wrote it because I was hearing so many teenagers and adults say goodbye by advising each other to "Be safe!" I made the case that admonishing each other to remember to guard our safety has nothing to do with Christ-following. I offered a list of alternate goodbye statements that communicate something more Jesus-centered. Here's a little sampler:

  Be Christ's! I remember an old story that J. Sidlow Baxter, the venerable English pastor and author, used to tell about a retired Scottish pastor he often passed on the lane near his home. Baxter once asked the old man, "How are you keeping?" The man responded, "I'm not keeping, I'm kept." Of all the things we can "be," nothing beats "Christ's."[47]

Stay awake! I think much of our culture is living life asleep at the wheel. That's one reason we see so many roadside wrecks in families today. Jesus told us to stay alert because there's a "roaring lion" stalking us. He wasn't kidding.

Be strong and courageous! When God placed the mantle of leadership on Joshua after Moses' death, he charged him to be "strong and courageous" three times in four verses (Joshua 1:6-9).

Be true! Rather than elevating safety as our filtering lens, how about reminding each other to speak and live the truth in every environment?

Live large! This one's a favorite of my friend Bob Krulish. Living small means to live disconnected from our true nature and calling; living large means to agree with Jesus about our place in his great rescue operation.

- **Games**—Not every game we play in youth ministry has to be specifically about Jesus. We're not playing Capture the Flag (With Jesus' Face on It). But if we're "saturating" kids with the beeline, I think it's great to look for the beeline to Jesus in every game we play and then use the game as a discussion starter or merely an example in a Jesus-centered conversation. This could be as simple as gathering at the end of every game in a huddle, then shouting together "Jesus was a gamer!" or something similar but less lame that fits your group's personality.

- **Conversations**—So how do we saturate our conversations with beelines to Jesus? I think the key is to listen well when teenagers tell us stories about their lives and then continually ask for more details. Try to find something in the student's conversation that would link to a Jesus-centered question or bridge. Some standard conversational Jesus-centered questions or bridges include:

"That reminds me so much of when Jesus said/did..."

"That's a tough one. Doesn't it make you wonder what Jesus would've done in your shoes?"

"This morning/afternoon/evening I was reading in one of the Gospels, and Jesus said/did something just like what you're talking about."

"I've learned something from Jesus about this..."

"If you'd invited him, do you think Jesus would have gone with you to do that?"

The first time you do this—like anything—it's pretty clunky. But the more often you practice, the more natural it becomes. Soon, it will be like breathing for you. The goal, remember, is to point back to Jesus in everything you do. Try it out first with your family, and play with it until you feel comfortable using it within your youth ministry.

- **Voice-mail messages**—Consider changing your voice-mail message every week to include a very short statement that replicates one of the alternate "goodbyes" I've listed earlier. For example, after your standard "I'm not here" message, simply close by saying "Be Christ's."

- **Emailing and text messaging**—When I return emails, I have a "signature" function that automatically gets added to the end of my messages. If you have the same feature, consider including a Jesus-centered message with your signature. For example: "I have determined to know nothing but Jesus Christ, and him crucified." Or if you're text messaging, consider signing each message with a Jesus-centered icon such as "4JC."

- **Meals**—How about surprising your students with alternative, Jesus-centered ways to say "grace" before your shared meals? Instead of bowing your heads and solemnly repeating your standard thanks for the food before you, what if you, instead, asked everyone to raise a glass to Jesus and then toasted him? What if you asked everyone to loudly whisper a cheer— "Jesus!"—all at the same time? What if you quoted a Jesus-centered Scripture passage such as: "Now to Him who is able to do far more abundantly beyond all that we ask or think, according to the power that works within us, to Him be the glory in the church and in Christ Jesus to all generations forever and ever. Amen" (Ephesians 3:20-21, NASB)?

The point, of course, is to teach ourselves to see the beeline in everything we do, and train others to do the same. That's saturation.

ENDNOTES

[1] Beth Moore, *Whispers of Hope: 10 Weeks of Devotional Prayer* (Nashville, TN: B&H Publishing Group, 2013), 83.

[2] Donald Miller, *Searching For God Knows What* (Nashville, TN: Thomas Nelson, 2004) 157-159. This is also the source for the previous, extended quote from Miller.

[3] Charles Sheldon, *In His Steps* (Uhrichsville, OH: Barbour Publishing, 2005).

[4] Scott Thumma, "A Health Checkup for U.S. Churches" by Hartford Institute for Religion Research (from a presentation at the Future of the Church Summit at Group Publishing, Loveland, Colorado, October 22, 2012).

[5] From the raw footage of videotaped interviews of teenagers across America, in 2005.

[6] To learn more about the *National Study of Youth and Religion,* go to youthandreligion.com or pick up Dr. Christian Smith's book (with Melinda Lundquist Denton) *Soul Searching: The Religious and Spiritual Lives of American Teenagers* (New York, NY: Oxford University Press, 2005).

7 From "Busting the Dropout Myth," by Tom Carpenter, Group Magazine, March/April 2007 issue.

8 From the report "Churchgoing In the UK," conducted by researchers with TearFund, published on the Why Church website (whychurch.org.uk).

9 From a sidebar titled "Whose Life Is It Anyway?" by Tim McTague, in the July 2006 issue of CCM Magazine.

10 From a Group Magazine survey of more than 10,000 Christian teenagers attending a Group Workcamp in the summer of 2006.

11 Eugene Peterson, from the foreword for *Jesus Mean and Wild: The Unexpected Love of an Untamable God* by Mark Galli (Grand Rapids, MI: Baker Books), 11.

12 Marshall McLuhan, *The Medium is the Massage* (Berkeley, CA: Gingko Press, 2001), 68.

13 From the infographic "Data Never Sleeps," compiled and posted by researchers at Domo.com.

14 Notes from a live presentation by Dr. David Walsh at the Cherry Creek School District Administrative Complex (Greenwood Village, Colorado) in May 2010.

15 From *The Young Turks*, first live Web-streamed and then uploaded on February 16, 2012.

16 N.T. Wright, *Following Jesus: Biblical Reflections on Discipleship* (Grand Rapids, MI: Eerdmans, 1994), ix.

17 From my own transcription of Peter Kreeft's lecture "The Shocking Beauty of Jesus," given at Gordon-Conwell Seminary on September 20, 2007, and later expanded upon in his book *Jesus-Shock* (St. Augustine's Press, 2008).

18 Brennan Manning, *Ruthless Trust* (New York, NY: Harper Collins Publishers, 2002), 88.

19 John Ortberg, *Who Is This Man?* (Grand Rapids, MI: Zondervan, 2012), 11-12.

20 Ned Erickson learned this progression from his ministry partners in Young Life.

21 The Exemplary Youth Ministries research project is a multi-denominational effort that produced a mountain of insight into effective youth ministry in the U.S.—my notes are from the original research report, but you can explore the results yourself by going to firstthird.org/eym/, or pick up a copy of *The Spirit and Culture of Youth Ministry* by Roland Martinson, Wesley Black, and John Roberto (EYM Publishing, August 29, 2012).

22 Matt Damon and Ben Affleck, *Good Will Hunting,* directed by Gus Von Sant (1997; Los Angeles: Walt Disney Video, 1999), DVD.

23 Taken from Sermon 242, *Christ Precious to Believers,* preached by Charles Spurgeon on March 13, 1859.

24 Quoted in *Spurgeon: Prince of Preachers,* by Lewis A. Drummond (Kregel Publications, 1992), 290.

25 Dr. Christian Smith quoted in the article "Youth Ministry's Impact!" in the May/June 2006 issue of Group Magazine.

26 Mark Galli, *Jesus Mean and Wild: The Unexpected Love of an Untamable God* (Grand Rapids, MI: Baker Books, 2006), 112.

27 C.S. Lewis, *The Lion, the Witch, and the Wardrobe* (New York, NY: Macmillan, 1950), 74-76.

28 This is from a prepared address by Harvard Law professor Mary Ann Glendon for the Pontifical Council for the Laity's 8th International Youth Forum, held near Rome in April 2004.

29 From a post on the website Concept to Classroom, in a workshop description titled "Inquiry-Based Learning (thirteen.org).

30 spurgeon.us/mind_and_heart/quotes/j.htm

[31] To learn more about the *Study of Exemplary Congregations in Youth Ministry,* go to exemplarym.com. The quotes from youth pastors, adult volunteers, senior pastors, and teenagers cited in the study throughout this book are taken from the study's in-site interviews.

[32] Information from the 24-7 Prayer Movement website at 24-7prayer.com.

[33] From notes taken at the Short-Term Missions Forum sponsored by the National Network of Youth and Religion, in January 2006.

[34] Taken from Appendix A of *Judaism For Dummies* by Rabbi Ted Falcon and David Blatner (New York, NY: Hungry Minds, Inc., 2001).

[35] This comment originally appeared in "The Do's and Don'ts of Youth-Led Ministry," from the September/October 2006 issue of Group Magazine.

[36] C.S. Lewis, *The Horse and His Boy,* (New York, NY: Macmillan, 1970), 158-159.

[37] C.S. Lewis, *The Voyage of the Dawn Treader* (New York, NY: Macmillan, 1970), 88-91.

[38] Read "The Tale of C.S. Lewis' Imaginative Legacy," by Dan DeWitt, published December 4, 2013, on the Southern Baptist Theological Seminary resources

page (sbts.edu/resources/towers/the-tale-of-c-s-lewis-imaginative-legacy/?utm_source=rss&utm_medium=rss&utm_campaign=the-tale-of-c-s-lewis-imaginative-legacy)

[39] From a story by Henri Nouwen in his book *The Road to Daybreak* (Image; Reissue edition, 1990).

[40] From "The Essential Guide to What Colors Communication," by Dustin W. Stout, posted on dustn.tv.

[41] From a Christianity Today interview of John Ortberg by Joe Carter, published September 18, 2012.

[42] Taken from vintage21.com.

[43] From a Colorado Public Radio report by Jenny Brundin titled "Science in Colorado Classrooms: Big Bang or Black Hole?—Part 1," first aired on October 5, 2012.

[44] Dialogue taken from the shooting script for *The Lord of the Rings: The Return of the King,* written by Fran Walsh, Philippa Boyens, and Peter Jackson, based on the book by J.R.R. Tolkien.

[45] Walter Wangerin, from a keynote address at Hutchmoot, an annual gathering organized by musician and author Andrew Peterson, August 2010.

[46] Taken from *Now Discover Your Strengths* by Marcus Buckingham and Donald O. Clifton (New York, NY: Free Press, 2001).

[47] From a sermon given by J. Sidlow Baxter at Calvary Temple Church in Denver, Colorado, in 1984.